what do we know and what should we do about...?

internet privacy

Paul Bernal

Los Angeles | London | New Delhi
Singapore | Washington DC | Melbourne

Los Angeles | London | New Delhi
Singapore | Washington DC | Melbourne

SAGE Publications Ltd
1 Oliver's Yard
55 City Road
London EC1Y 1SP

SAGE Publications Inc.
2455 Teller Road
Thousand Oaks, California 91320

SAGE Publications India Pvt Ltd
B 1/I 1 Mohan Cooperative Industrial Area
Mathura Road
New Delhi 110 044

SAGE Publications Asia-Pacific Pte Ltd
3 Church Street
#10-04 Samsung Hub
Singapore 049483

Editor: Matthew Waters
Editorial assistant: Jasleen Kaur
Production editor: Katherine Haw
Copyeditor: Neville Hankins
Proofreader: Clare Weaver
Indexer: Charmian Parkin
Marketing manager: George Kimble
Cover design: Lisa Harper-Wells
Typeset by: C&M Digitals (P) Ltd, Chennai, India
Printed in the UK

© Paul Bernal 2020

First published 2020

Apart from any fair dealing for the purposes of research or private study, or criticism or review, as permitted under the Copyright, Designs and Patents Act, 1988, this publication may be reproduced, stored or transmitted in any form, or by any means, only with the prior permission in writing of the publishers, or in the case of reprographic reproduction, in accordance with the terms of licences issued by the Copyright Licensing Agency. Enquiries concerning reproduction outside those terms should be sent to the publishers.

Library of Congress Control Number: 2019956625

British Library Cataloguing in Publication data

A catalogue record for this book is available from the British Library

ISBN 978-1-5297-0768-7
ISBN 978-1-5297-0767-0 (pbk)

At SAGE we take sustainability seriously. Most of our products are printed in the UK using responsibly sourced papers and boards. When we print overseas we ensure sustainable papers are used as measured by the PREPS grading system. We undertake an annual audit to monitor our sustainability.

contents

About the series v

About the author vii

1 Introduction 1

2 Background 15

3 What do we know? 31

4 What should we do? 63

5 Conclusions 73

Further reading and references 75

Index 79

titles in the series

What Do We Know and What Should We Do About Immigration?
Jonathan Portes

What Do We Know and What Should We Do About Inequality?
Mike Brewer

What Do We Know and What Should We Do About the Future of Work?
Melanie Simms

What Do We Know and What Should We Do About Housing?
Rowland Atkinson and Keith Jacobs

Forthcoming:

What Do We Know and What Should We Do About Terrorism?
Brooke Rogers

What Do We Know and What Should We Do About Sustainable Living?
Kate Burningham and Tim Jackson

What Do We Know and What Should We Do About Fake News?
Nick Anstead

What Do We Know and What Should We Do About Slavery?
Julia O'Connell-Davidson

What Do We Know and What Should We Do About Social Mobility?
Lee Elliot Major and Stephen Machin

about the series

Every news bulletin carries stories which relate in some way to the social sciences – most obviously politics, economics and sociology but also, often, anthropology, business studies, security studies, criminology, geography and many others.

Yet despite the existence of large numbers of academics who research these subjects, relatively little of their work is known to the general public. There are many reasons for that but one, arguably, is that the kinds of formats that social scientists publish in, and the way in which they write, are simply not accessible to the general public.

The guiding theme of this series is to provide a format and a way of writing which addresses this problem. Each book in the series is concerned with a topic of widespread public interest, and each is written in a way which is readily understandable to the general reader with no particular background knowledge.

The authors are academics with an established reputation and a track record of research in the relevant subject. They provide an overview of the research knowledge about the subject, whether this be long-established or reporting the most recent findings; widely accepted or still controversial. Often in public debate there is a demand for greater clarity about the facts, and that is one of the things the books in this series provide.

However, in social sciences, facts are often disputed and subject to different interpretations. They do not always, or even often, 'speak for themselves'. The authors therefore strive to show the different interpretations or the key controversies about their topics, but without getting bogged down in arcane academic arguments.

Not only can there be disputes about facts but also there are almost invariably different views on what should follow from these facts. And, in any case, public debate requires more of academics than just to report facts; it is also necessary to make suggestions and recommendations about the implications of these facts.

Thus each volume also contains ideas about 'what we should do' within each topic area. These are based upon the authors' knowledge of the field but also, inevitably, upon their own views, values and preferences. Readers may not agree with them, but the intention is to provoke thought and well-informed debate.

Chris Grey, Series Editor

Professor of Organization Studies

Royal Holloway, University of London

about the author

Paul Bernal is Associate Professor of IT, IP and Media Law at the UEA Law School, University of East Anglia, UK. His research focuses on privacy and other human rights on the internet and the role of social media. He blogs, tweets and contributes to journalism on these and many other related areas – and even occasionally writes poetry.

introduction

From something that even a few years ago was largely the province of only a few geeks and nerds, internet privacy has more recently become a subject of interest to pretty much everyone. In 2013, Edward Snowden made surveillance by governments headline news across the globe. The way that what we browse and search for on the internet is used to target advertisements to us – sometimes with disturbingly creepy precision, at other times with almost humorous inaccuracy – and is something with which we are all familiar. The possibility that we are being manipulated through Facebook – indeed that we *have already* been manipulated through Facebook, with potentially devastating consequences for our whole democratic system – is quite another matter, and one that people seem to find very difficult to face up to.

This book will try to unpick some key questions relating to all of this and more. It will argue that internet privacy – or, to be more precise, addressing our failure to properly protect privacy on the internet – is critical for our future in a wide range of ways – ways that we generally fundamentally misunderstand. We worry about things that we really don't need to, and don't worry about things that we really should. We willingly enable things that undermine our autonomy and democracy, primarily because we don't see the consequences of what we are doing. This needs to change, and needs to change soon if we are to find a way forward that protects the things that we really care about.

In order to find this way, we need to examine the key questions. Should we be more worried about government surveillance or corporate data gathering? Is it necessary to sacrifice our privacy in order to get more security – accepting government surveillance, for example, to protect our society from terrorism, children from paedophiles and vulnerable citizens from scammers and fraudsters? Is the current model of data gathering, profiling and micro-targeting the best way to sustain our 'free' access to social media, email and the wonderful information source that is the World Wide Web? Is the convenience offered by the so-called 'internet of things' – from smart cars and smart fridges to voice-activated 'smart speakers' – worth the consequences to our privacy? And, perhaps most importantly, if people don't seem to *care* about their privacy – and by their actions rather than their words, it can be argued that they don't – then why should anything be done about it at all?

The answers to some of these questions often seem obvious – at least to governments, and often to the media – but things are rarely as simple as they seem. Many of the questions themselves are based on misconceptions and misunderstandings. In practice, for example, considering government and corporate surveillance as separate and different is to misunderstand the whole nature of both government surveillance and the business models prevalent on the internet. Authorities 'piggyback' on data gathering systems run by businesses, use profiling tools created for advertising, and learn who people are communicating with by monitoring their social media activity.

Similarly, the idea of balancing privacy and security is a damaging oversimplification. Very often, making compromises to privacy actually reduces our security – undermining encryption systems by mandating 'back doors' for the authorities is a prime example but far from the only one. Excessive surveillance can encourage the development of countermeasures, both technical and practical, that end up making it easier for well-skilled operatives to evade the authorities. A requirement for 'real names', though on the face of it providing more security and protection against trolls and stalkers, can in practice have the opposite effect and make exactly the people it is supposed to protect *more* vulnerable rather than less and make it easier for the real trolls to find and harm their victims. There are similar issues in almost every area – and as the internet now pervades almost every aspect of our lives, that has very significant implications.

The internet

The 'network of networks' (which is what 'internet' really means) began through military and academic projects in the late 1960s and early 1970s and has become a critical part of the infrastructure of our education systems, our businesses, our governments and much more. Many of the biggest companies in the world are in effect *internet* companies – not just Google and Facebook, but Amazon, Apple and Microsoft, and, in China, Tencent and Alibaba. The internet reaches into all of our technology – not just our communications and information sources, but our cars, energy and heating, our televisions and music.

Our calendars are online, our fitness is monitored online, we shop, find jobs and date online. We book our travel and entertainment online. It is hard to find a part of our lives that does *not* have a significant online element. Because of the nature of the internet, this means that we leave a trail, a record of our actions, in the form of data. This data by *its* nature can be used for analysis, for profiling, for aggregation, to create more data, and to *predict* more potential information about almost everything. From a privacy perspective this is important because it means that the information available through our connections and actions on the internet can be used to discover a vast amount about us in all kinds of ways.

In historical terms this is unprecedented, which in turn means that the implications of it are hard to understand. The title of this book series is 'What Do We Know About…?' but perhaps the most important thing to 'know' about internet privacy and the ramifications of our inability or failure to protect it is that in many ways we really *don't* know as much about internet privacy as we should. There are a vast number of things that we do know about it, but the possible consequences are only just beginning to become clear. The 'unknown unknowns', as Donald Rumsfeld might have put it, may be the biggest concern of all.

Privacy

Defining what exactly is meant by privacy has been a challenge for scholars for many years – some scholars suggest that the very attempt to pin down a definition may be not just futile but counterproductive. Any definition would be likely to exclude some things that we *feel* to be privacy and include things that do not have that quality. In their seminal paper of 1890,

'The right to privacy', Warren and Brandeis set it out as a 'right to be let alone', but their paper was primarily triggered by intrusion by the press into the private lives of the social elite and reflects that quite directly.

The idea of privacy has been central to *human rights* law since the start but again without any precise definition. The Universal Declaration of Human Rights, adopted by the new United Nations in 1948, in the aftermath of the Second World War and the Holocaust, included in Article 12 that '[n]o one shall be subjected to arbitrary interference with his privacy, family, home or correspondence' but did not offer any definition for privacy to clarify. The European Convention on Human Rights, signed by the Council of Europe, included as Article 8 that '[e]veryone has the right to respect for his private and family life, his home and his correspondence' but again failed to define what was meant by 'private' life.

These latter two elements, 'home' and 'correspondence', form two of the key elements that have historically been considered private both in common terms and in law. 'An Englishman's home is his castle' points to the common understanding while the protection against what in the United States would be called 'unreasonable search and seizure', set out in the Fourth Amendment to its Constitution in 1791, is a prime example of the legal.

The importance of police and others being unable to enter your home without a warrant is a key element of living in a 'free' country rather than a police state – listening to phone calls and opening letters are considered classical intrusions into privacy. Indeed, it is all too common that when governments are discovered to be invading people's privacy in other ways for officials to say 'we're not listening to your phone calls' or 'we're not reading your emails' primarily as a supposed reassurance to cover up what are, in practice, even more intrusive actions.

Privacy of correspondence has another critical element, one that has been reflected in law and in particular in the law of England and Wales: *confidence*. Correspondence is one thing, *confidential* correspondence is another level. In law the idea that you can have a confidential relationship that requires and inspires a 'higher level' of privacy has existed for centuries at least. Relationships like doctor–patient, client–lawyer, constituent–MP and, on a slightly different angle, spouse–spouse have been given special protection, as have those between diplomats and other government representatives.

Confidentiality in business negotiations is considered crucial. Quite what constitutes a confidential relationship is not precisely or easily defined – there have been arguments in court about things like the relationships between prostitutes and their clients – but that *confidentiality* itself exists and is important is not in doubt and *breaches* of confidentiality have often been seen as legally actionable.

The idea of a private, *confidential* relationship demonstrates that privacy is 'relational': what matters is who you need privacy *from*. When considering surveillance, we are often considering privacy from the authorities. 'Big brother is watching you' expresses one of the classical fears of privacy invasion. When looking at the roles of Google and Facebook, it is privacy from *corporations* that is the most obvious concern. A victim of stalking needs privacy from their stalker. A whistle-blower needs privacy from their employer. A celebrity may need privacy from the press. A child may need privacy from their parents.

So, we have places that are private – in particular the home – and correspondence being private. We have relationships that are private. What we also have is *information* that is private. Precisely what kind of information counts as private depends on a number of things, but subjects like health, sexuality, political views and religion are almost universally considered to be both *private* and *personal*. Other information, for example financial status and tax affairs, is generally considered private but in some places that may not be the case. In Norway, for example, tax returns are public documents and available online through a searchable database.

In specific circumstances, many other things are considered private – you may not want to reveal who you work for to everyone, for example. Your address may sometimes be public – available on the electoral roll, for example – but may also be kept private and is certainly personal. Importantly, what matters for one person may not matter for another. Almost anything can potentially be considered both personal and private for particular people in particular circumstances – from something as direct as what football team they support or what bands they enjoy to things like the kind of food they eat or what they buy at the supermarket. This idea, that of *informational privacy*, is one of the key ideas to understand in relation to the internet.

Informational privacy

In the 1960s, legal scholar Alan Westin took us another step forward in understanding privacy in the new context, suggesting that privacy is about *information*. He defined privacy as 'the claim of individuals, groups, or institutions to determine for themselves when, how, and to what extent information about them is communicated to others' – a definition that has more direct relevance to the context of the internet, it being a medium for the communication of information. It captures the *relational* aspect of privacy – the 'privacy from whom' element – and the *autonomy* aspect, the way in which it is about both freedom and control.

Even it, however, does not really capture the nature of privacy in all its aspects, particularly in the online environment. Does the act of being monitored involve the communication of information? Does the *possibility* of being monitored involve the communication of information? Both of these involve invasions of privacy – and the differences between them, and between them and the Westin definition, hint at one of the critical questions that will be returned to a number of times in this book: when does privacy 'kick in', and hence when does any *protection* for privacy need to be applied? Consider, for example, a digital CCTV camera set up to look into a person's home. Is the privacy invasion when the camera is installed? When it is turned on? When the footage is recorded? When it is automatically analysed and the footage when there is movement within is filtered out? When it is algorithmically analysed to compare to a facial recognition database? Or when that information is presented to a human being for scrutiny?

Historically, in terms of both law and ethics, arguments have been made for each of these kinds of stages. The European Court of Human Rights has suggested that even establishing a law that would allow the setting up of systems to monitor people would engage our human rights, while it is a fairly regular suggestion from security advocates that nothing really matters until human beings are involved, so that it is only at that stage that (a) anyone needs to worry and (b) there needs to be any kind of serious accountability.

In practice, as many of the examples used in this book will demonstrate, the European Court of Human Rights has a much stronger argument than the authorities – and even then it does not go far enough to understand the breadth and depth of the issues. Further, law is only a small part of the story. We need to be concerned about technology that might even allow privacy invasions to be possible, regardless of the legality. Almost all aspects of the internet in its current form fit into this category.

Downplaying privacy...

Though privacy has a key role in human rights law and has been actionable in various ways for a long time, there has also been a tendency to downplay its importance and its history. It is sometimes portrayed as a luxury and an indulgence – something that should be overridden when needed, often by other 'more important' rights and needs, from security to freedom of expression, to the 'need' for businesses to make money. It is portrayed as an individual issue, in opposition to collective and hence more important things – again, the regular comparisons are with security and economic success. That makes privacy even appear to be *selfish* – and used as a kind of moral argument for the abandonment of privacy in the face of far more important things.

Connected with this, privacy is also sometimes described as a kind of historical anomaly, a current indulgence. We didn't have it in the past and we won't have it in the future: we only want it now because we're comfortable in other ways. They didn't have privacy in the Middle Ages, let alone further back than that, this logic suggests. In the other direction, it is often suggested that privacy won't exist in the future – or indeed that it is already dead, either having been killed by technology or having been abandoned by the new generations. 'You have zero privacy anyway, get over it' was what then CEO of Sun Microsystems, Scott McNealy, told a room full of journalists in 1999 – and that was before the development of social media or the mass surveillance systems of the NSA, GCHQ and others.

Mark Zuckerberg, the main founder of Facebook, suggested in 2010 that privacy was no longer a social norm, while former Amazon chief scientist Andreas Weigend gave his 2017 book on the big data economy the subtitle 'How to make our post-privacy economy work for you'. This subtitle hints at one of the other related narratives regarding privacy: that we should abandon it and take the opportunities that its abandonment might provide. Privacy really doesn't matter that much, according to this narrative, and we've lost it anyway, so we should embrace the new, privacy-free environment.

None of these attempts to downplay the importance of privacy are really true and none of them are fair. Privacy is not a luxury or an indulgence and neither is it 'individual' in any real sense. In practice, privacy is most often about *relationships*: that 'correspondence' has always been central to privacy law gives a big clue to how it works. Privacy underpins communities, and privacy is needed to enable other key rights rather than existing in opposition to them. A journalist needs confidentiality for their sources. An intimate relationship needs privacy to work at all. The security and intelligence services themselves *rely* on privacy and confidentiality to do their jobs. Businesses need confidentiality of information to function. Without privacy all these things are broken.

A more careful study of history does not support the idea that privacy is something new. Though the label and language may not be as clear in the past, the *concept* and *practice* of privacy has a very long history indeed – particularly, but not exclusively, in relation to the two key elements mentioned above: home and correspondence. The idea that a home should be protected has existed in almost all cultures across the world and throughout history – bolstered by ideas such as sanctuary for people in churches and temples.

The struggle for confidentiality of communications has just as long a history – the idea of encryption for messages, for example, reaches back as far as the ancient Greeks at least, and by the time of the Elizabethans was already highly sophisticated. Whole languages were developed with the primary function of keeping communications private – the notorious *thieves' argot* developed some time in the sixteenth century is just one example.

The converse idea, that young people no longer care about privacy – evidenced, in the eyes of Mark Zuckerberg at least, by the fact that they *share* masses of personal information that people in the past might have considered private – is similarly misconceived. When looked at closely, as a number of scholars have done, it can be seen that young people do indeed care about privacy, just in a different way than their predecessors. Indeed, in many ways, as shall be shown later in this book, they care *more* about privacy than some of their elders, engage better with privacy-protective technology, and are more 'savvy' about how to avoid being monitored and manipulated via the internet. Young people, for example, are less likely to be fooled by *fake news* than those of middle age and above.

What is also worth noticing is that almost all of those who seek to downplay privacy have something of a vested interest in that downplaying. The security and intelligence services would benefit if we all gave up privacy, and let them intrude on us at all times – or at least they believe they would benefit, for as we shall see later it is something of an illusion that giving up privacy is really of a benefit to security. The likes of McNealy and

Zuckerberg – and indeed Weigend – would prefer there to be no restrictions on their businesses' extraction and use of personal data, so that they can make as much money as possible. If they can convince the authorities that protecting privacy is not necessary, their opportunities are thus far less restricted. This means at the very least that we should take these attempts to downplay privacy with a distinct pinch of salt.

There is another way that privacy can be downplayed – through the use of language. This has a number of dimensions. Sometimes the word *confidentiality* is used to substitute for privacy. Though the concepts are related, confidentiality is a much more limited concept than privacy and can reduce the apparent importance. A breach in confidentiality can be seen more as a 'faux pas' or something that might be embarrassing, or perhaps damage the business interests of the rich, rather than as a breach of human rights or something with broad implications for freedom and autonomy. Confidentiality is about trust rather than about autonomy.

Even worse is the substitution of the word *secrecy*. Secrecy directly implies some kind of *hiding* and can have even darker implications. Using the term also brings another classical privacy canard, the often repeated 'if you've got nothing to hide you've got nothing to fear' into play and along with it all the misleading questions of balance that it brings.

Nothing to hide?

The 'nothing to hide' suggestion is persistent, misleading and manipulative. It is used not just to justify government surveillance but press intrusion into the personal lives of celebrities, politicians and indeed the public. It takes downplaying privacy to another level: good people, according to this logic, don't *need* privacy, as they have nothing to hide, while bad people don't *deserve* privacy, so as we're all either good or bad, *no one* should have privacy. Indeed, it become almost a public duty to invade privacy, for both the authorities and the press, and claiming privacy automatically makes you suspicious. Privacy advocates become the friends – perhaps the 'useful idiots' – of criminals and terrorists, paedophiles and drug dealers.

On the surface, the 'nothing to hide' argument is attractive and there is an underlying point: rogues of all sorts *will* use privacy protections where they are available. However, it is also a fundamentally flawed argument in a number of ways and has been taken apart by privacy scholars for many years. There are a number of direct responses available to people making the argument:

> If you have nothing to hide, why do you have curtains?
>
> I don't have anything to hide, but I don't have anything I feel like showing you either.
>
> It's not about having anything to hide, it's about things not being anyone else's business.
>
> If you don't have anything to hide, then you don't have a life.

This last one may seem flippant but it is making a critical point. Details of anyone's life, should they do anything interesting at all, can potentially be used against them, used to manipulate them, used out of context, misunderstood either deliberately or unintentionally. As Cardinal Richelieu is said to have put it, 'If you give me six lines written by the hand of the most honest of men, I will find something in them which will hang him.'

The flaws in the 'nothing to hide' argument arise because it is based on a fundamental misunderstanding of the nature of privacy. Privacy isn't just about 'bad' things and it isn't about 'hiding' so much as about autonomy and some degree of control. Often the most private things are the most precious and the most intimate, not the kind of dark secrets or bad stories that this logic supposes.

Moreover, the 'nothing to hide' argument makes an assumption that those who will get access to the 'secrets' are doing so for positive reasons. A 'good' government seeking to fight crime and prevent terrorism. A 'noble' press seeking to root out rogues and charlatans in public life. Positive corporations seeking to improve their products and services for the benefit of their customers and the economy. History should teach us that though these good governments, noble journalists and beneficent corporations do exist, it is foolish to assume that all are like that and the 'nothing to hide' argument falls apart when the oppressive governments, intrusive press and exploitative corporations get involved. Further, there are very few governments, press enterprises or corporations that do not have at least some oppressive, intrusive or exploitative tendencies or people involved with such tendencies.

One more linguistic angle is how the people claiming privacy are described. Sometimes, particularly in the context of commercial invasions of privacy, people are referred to as 'consumers'. In 2012, President Obama introduced to great fanfare a 'Consumer Privacy Bill of Rights' just a few months before Edward Snowden revealed that under Obama's presidency the US intelligence and security services had built up a system that had put pretty much the entire internet under intense surveillance.

By considering privacy a *consumer* issue, government surveillance is downplayed: it is not as *consumers* that we might object to government surveillance. Sometimes privacy is seen as a civil or *citizen*'s right but this too undervalues privacy as it effectively gives governments free rein in relation to non-citizens and in particular immigrants. It is notable that in the UK's most recent data protection law, the Data Protection Act 2018, there is a carve-out allowing authorities to override this key form of privacy protection when dealing with immigration. The language used in relation to privacy matters: privacy should be seen primarily as a *human* right rather than either a consumer right or a civil right. Each of those aspects is relevant in its own right but they can be used to limit protection, to excuse particular forms of intrusion, and to shift the focus away from other key issues.

The problem of harm...

One further way in which privacy can be downplayed and misunderstood, particularly in the internet context, is through a focus on the 'harm' that an invasion of privacy causes. The law of 'tort' (civil rather than criminal 'wrongs') historically allowed one person to sue another for an injury or *harm* that other person might have done to them. If you damage someone's property or their reputation, for example, they might be able to bring an action against you, to sue you for the damage caused. These actions generally (and appropriately) require the damage to be in some way proven and measurable or at least assessable.

Privacy law has generally fitted into this category but that makes things very difficult in a number of ways, and is one reason that historically there has been no tort of privacy in the law of England and Wales. In some other jurisdictions it is a little different but the difficulty remains. In US law, as Calo puts it, '[a] privacy harm must be "cognizable," "actual," "specific," "material," "fundamental," or "special" before a court will consider awarding compensation'. This makes the effect of privacy invasion difficult to assess in any context: the emotional damage of a privacy invasion and the impact on dignity are not easy to assess.

All of this is even more difficult to prove in relation to the kinds of problems caused by privacy in the internet context. The harm caused by gathering personal data on an individual is very hard to measure – and may *individually* have no measurable effect at all. In a legal sense, no direct *harm* at all. Applying this kind of logic has led some to suggest that privacy harm is not really a harm at all, or if it is a harm, this harm is really insignificant and hence should be ignored in relation to the benefits that the privacy invasion allows, whether they be to security for governments or innovation or economic benefits for commercial operators.

'Where's the harm in this?' is an easy question to ask and not an easy one to answer, but is one that must be answered and must be better understood. The *harms* from privacy invasion on the internet, as is discussed in detail throughout this book, come more from the big picture than the individual incidents. The cumulative effect of tiny acts of individual data gathering allows profiling that can produce harms not associated with any of those individual acts.

Privacy invasions on one person can also have an impact on others: the nature of profiling is that it looks at the *kind* of person that the data might relate to. As an individual, you might protect yourself from data gathering, avoid Facebook, use privacy-friendly search engines and encrypt your messages, but because enough people are *not* doing so, a profile can be built up about you based on the data of those others. The more data there is on all people the less that is needed on each individual in order to profile them. An environment where privacy is not properly protected and is not properly valued has an impact on our autonomy, our community, our ability to function with others, our ability to participate in democracy and more. The focus on harms, and on the individual events, therefore, is to miss the main context of privacy on the internet.

That then sets the scene. The rest of this book will try to explain first of all how the internet came to be what it is today and why privacy is such a key issue for so many aspects of it. It will do so first of all through a historical analysis, charting the development of the internet from a niche, technical system to an all-pervading network underpinning most aspects of our lives. This analysis will include the key developments – the World

Wide Web, search, social networking and big data analysis – and the role of government surveillance, and how all of these relate *directly* to privacy. It will then move on to a discussion of where we are now – how the current manifestation of the internet works for people, for companies and for governments, using examples from familiar situations including shopping and social networking. Then there will be a look at the new privacy battlefields of location data, health data, facial recognition and other biometrics, the internet of things and the increasingly contentious issue of political data and political manipulation – and at the legal, technological and practical protections that exist to provide some degree of respite from the multifarious threats to our privacy.

That the last main section of the book, on what we should do about the problems surrounding internet privacy, is shorter than the section on where we are is a reflection of the current state of affairs: there *are* a vast array of threats and it *is* difficult to see ways to address them. Part of the challenge right now is to understand that basic problem, because until we understand it we are unlikely to take the big, radical steps that may be necessary. These include significant changes in government policies – reversing the current 'war' on encryption and challenging the idea that 'real names' would improve the discourse on social networks – as well as being brave enough to take on the internet giants, and seriously considering the break-up of Facebook in particular. These are challenging ideas but as this book will argue, they may well be necessary.

background

A very, very brief history of the internet – from a privacy perspective

Privacy, as has been shown, is not simple and is rarely properly understood. It is an issue with a long history and one which is hard to pin down. It has broad implications, getting broader all the time in our current information-based society. It has complex and often paradoxical interactions and tensions with a wide range of other issues and rights, from security and freedom of expression to the rights and needs of businesses to operate successfully. This is all brought into focus in the specific context of the internet: to understand how and why, we need to look at the history and nature of the internet itself.

The internet could be said to have *emerged* rather than have been created. It grew from Joseph Licklider's early work in connecting computers at MIT, from which he was brought into the US government's 'Advanced Research Projects Agency' (ARPA), in the 1960s. At ARPA, Licklider built the 'ARPANET', which incorporated several of the key aspects of what would later become the internet. These included 'packet-switching' – effectively, breaking down data into small 'packets' which are sent independently and individually from one place to another, possibly travelling different routes to the destination, where they are put back together into their original form.

They also included the need for all computers on the network to be 'compatible' with each other – following the same rules, understanding the same instructions – in order to communicate with each other. ARPANET, however, was a single and effectively 'closed' network. It set some of the rules and established some of the underlying principles behind what emerged later, but was very different indeed from the vast and open 'network of networks' that we now know as the internet. That grew from the work of the likes of Bob Kahn, Vint Cerf and others, who set about finding ways to link networks internationally, taking advantage of a number of different technological developments in the 1970s, including the growing network of communications satellites. They found a solution to the compatibility issue through the development of the *Transmission Control Protocol* which developed into the *Transmission Control Protocol/Internet Protocol* ('TCP/IP') which is still how the internet works today. TCP breaks the data into packets, while IP deals with the addressing and routing of the packets from their transmission point to the desired destination (the *IP address*).

All this may seem rather technical and not tremendously relevant to the internet as it functions today, but from a privacy perspective it is critical. *Data packets* are effectively put into digital 'envelopes' labelled with the IP address, and as it was first set up, what was actually *in* the envelopes was irrelevant and effectively *unknown* to the network, or any of the points on the network through which the envelopes passed. Further, as each individual packet made up only a tiny part of the original data, and as each packet travelled its own route to the destination, the overall 'message' would be very hard to identify through each packet. To get the whole message you would need to find each of the packets, then find a way to put them all together into a decipherable form, which would take a lot of effort and expertise. With speed, simplicity and compatibility as priorities and a relatively homogeneous and trusting community, putting significant effort into breaking that privacy was highly unlikely to happen, at least in the early days of the internet.

As a consequence, the internet in its original form offered a good deal of practical protection for privacy at least in terms of *communication*. Communication in its conventional form, however, was only the beginning of what the internet made possible.

This basic protection was part of what led to the early ideas of privacy and anonymity on the internet, and hence to the characterisation of the internet set out in the seminal 1993 cartoon in the *New Yorker*, 'On the Internet, nobody knows you're a dog' (Figure 2.1).

background

"On the Internet, nobody knows you're a dog."

Figure 2.1
Image courtesy of www.CartoonCollections.com

How we got from that form of privacy and effective anonymity to the current internet where it appears at least that companies and governments know more about you than you know yourself is important to understand. It is not just about the technology – though a basic understanding of the technology really helps – but about two other key factors.

First of all, it is about *who* is on the internet. In the early days, it was primarily geeks and nerds, working in universities or government institutions.

A relatively homogeneous group – mostly male, white, rich, educated and American – with what were effectively very similar and relatively compatible needs and purposes. Now, it is almost everybody, almost every business, group, school, church, government institution, political pressure group, political party, criminal group, and many more. It even includes increasing numbers of *things*, from connected cars to 'smart TVs' and even 'smart' roads and cities.

The change in those who use the internet has a profound effect on the way that privacy can or should be dealt with. The original group largely trusted one another and felt each other were worthy of trust. They had similar or at least compatible views of privacy and accepted the ideas of anonymity (or pseudonymity) shown in the *New Yorker* cartoon in part because of that. They could identify each other in other ways anyway and did not feel threatened by each other – they had neither the motivation nor the inclination to try to exploit each other through invasions of privacy, at least for the main part. As the internet has grown, all of that has changed. Now that it encompasses almost half the people on the planet, very much the opposite is true in almost all these ways. Attitudes vary massively. People feel threatened – and people *are* threatened – by others in a wide variety of ways. People are being exploited and others seek to exploit and manipulate people on a grand scale, for a wide range of motives from the personal and financial to the political and criminal.

Second, it is about *how* the people, groups, companies and government bodies use the internet. The internet began as simple communication – email was the first key function – and evolved through being an information resource, then a place for socialising, to something that now underpins almost all our activities. When the internet was just for email or access to information, privacy was relatively simple and the motivations for invading it were clear and relatively easily defended against. As the functions to which we put the internet have developed, so have the threats to privacy.

Key moments in this development include the invention of the World Wide Web, the emergence of Google and the development of search and the business model around it, Facebook and the social media explosion – the emergence of what is referred to as 'surveillance capitalism' – the growth of 'big data' and the massive expansion of government surveillance as we learned through the revelations of Edward Snowden, all of which will be discussed in more depth below. None of these should be considered in isolation: there is a close relationship between all of them. They feed on one another and understanding *that* is critical to understanding the nature of the threats to our privacy, the implications of those threats and what we can do to address them.

There is a third factor that needs to be taken into account – another key aspect of the development of the internet from the province of nerds to something that involves everyone. This is the relationship between the *online* world and the 'real' world. In the early days of the internet 'cyberspace' was seen as a separate realm, independent and unconnected from the 'real' world. In 1996, John Perry Barlow wrote his 'Declaration of the Independence of Cyberspace', telling governments that '…the global social space we are building to be naturally independent of the tyrannies you seek to impose on us. You have no moral right to rule us nor do you possess any methods of enforcement we have true reason to fear.' Barlow's declaration resonates with many still, despite the fallacy at the heart of it: no matter what you do online, your physical body still exists and exists in the jurisdiction of a 'real-world' government and that physical body can have law enforced upon it.

This fallacy – or to be more exact the way of bringing the fallacy into reality – is one of the keys to understanding privacy on the internet. One of the main motivations behind invasions of privacy is to make the link between someone's online identity and their 'real-world' identity and hence their physical body. A government wants to enforce criminal law online. A bully wants to physically find their victim. A business wants to sell something in the real world through its presence online – or find customers near their physical location. In order to do any of these things they all need to be able to make that link between the online and offline worlds. Conversely, anyone who wants their online activity *not* to be linked to their physical existence needs to be able to protect themselves: dissidents avoiding oppressive governments, abused spouses avoiding their abusers, whistle-blowers not wanting to be discovered by their employers and more.

As the online and offline worlds have become more and more integrated, dealing with the online/offline links has become one of the key privacy battlefields. From requiring 'real names' on social media to giving law enforcement access to the location of mobile phones, from facial recognition in CCTV cameras to providing social media data when you cross borders or apply for visas, a great many issues ultimately boil down to ways to pin down an online identity in the physical world. This is a more complex issue than it seems: supposedly simple solutions such as using real names to prevent trolling often end up not just failing but actually being damagingly counterproductive.

The internet and the World Wide Web

Perhaps the single most important step in the transformation of the internet from an obscure tool for geeks and nerds to the all-pervasive network that underpins all our lives was the development of the *World Wide Web* (more simply *the web*). Developed in the late 1980s by Briton Tim Berners-Lee at *CERN* in Switzerland, the web made information on the internet more accessible, more attractive, more *usable* and more navigable. Providing a way to present data – the web page – and to *link* between one page and another, through clickable hyperlinks, transformed the internet in its function as an information resource, as well as paving the way to all kinds of new and different uses for the net.

For many people, the web *is* the internet – indeed, the words are used almost interchangeably by a great many (including those who should know better). This has changed somewhat in more recent times, as the use of mobile devices has begun to dominate access to the internet, and with it the use of *apps* rather than web browsers, but many apps are essentially interfaces to access web pages and the structure of the web remains the key. It did not just make information more accessible and useful, it established the idea that the internet should be a user-friendly resource for a mass audience, not just for those technically educated and skilled. That in turn paved the way for the use of the net for many different *kinds* of information: if all kinds of people are using the web, then far more different resources could find an audience there. The mass expansion of the internet became possible and practical.

Search and destroy?

So much information started to appear on the web that finding your way through it became a critical task – both for those seeking information and for those who wanted to have their information found. Before the emergence of Google in the late 1990s, search was a simple affair, only about navigating the rapidly growing quantities of information. It had not really been seen as a business proposition, nor had any effective business model been built around it – indeed, business itself was not a key part of the internet. Google changed all of that. Yes, it was about navigating the internet and it did that part really well, better than any system before, but it was about much more than that. The way that it did it changed almost everything about the way the internet worked, particularly insofar as privacy was concerned.

Google didn't just find you what you needed on the internet, it made money by doing so, and *both* parts of that involved the gathering and analysis of information – including private and personal information – on a grand scale. Search terms are gathered and analysed, to know how many people are searching for what – and, ultimately, *which* people are searching for what – and then which links they are following. By this, Google maps out not just what is on the internet – the websites – but the people on the internet, their behaviour, their habits and much more. Precisely which data is gathered has changed over the years as the technology has developed and the opportunities have grown. The data is gathered in a way that is far from clear for the user. Google's interface is very simple: an almost blank page with a single box in the middle for you to enter your search term. Nothing says that data is being gathered, that a log of search terms, a *search history*, is being generated, that the user is being *profiled*. Google did not start this kind of profiling but it built a business model upon it and changed the nature of the internet fundamentally.

Google's business model used this profiling to target advertising, initially that surrounded the search results. This grew into an advertising business that dominated not only in online advertising but *all* advertising. The spectacular success of this advertising model depended primarily on two things. First of all, providing a service that really worked and met the needs of the users. Second, on being able to target sufficiently accurately to meet the needs of the advertisers, and that depended on the quality of the profiling. That in turn depended on the quantity and quality of the data gathered and the ability to analyse that data. Google did this in a way and on a scale that had never been attempted before, taking advantage of the very nature of the internet and of the people who use it.

In privacy terms this has a number of implications. Knowing what people are searching for on the internet is itself a privacy invasion: we search for some of the most intimate and sensitive things, from medical symptoms to sexuality, when we're looking for jobs and more. Profiling takes this a step further, gaining 'insights' that might well be a deeper invasion of privacy. People might be a little reticent about directly searching for some things, but if the profiling systems are able to *derive* those sensitive things from more mundane information searched for, that would enable privacy invasion anyway. The ability to *target* people based on the profiling is another dimension in privacy invasion.

The ability to *tailor* services can take this to another level. *Tailoring* or *personalisation* is the key to some of the most dangerous and damaging effects of our failure to protect privacy, particularly if it happens without the person for whom a service is being tailored realising it. A product or service could be offered to someone not at the price it is offered to anyone else but at the maximum price that profiling suggests they would be prepared to pay. Products that you *need* can be made more expensive, while products that you don't need can be made more attractive based on your profile to make you more likely to buy them. Products or services that might be better suited to you but cheaper can be concealed from you. The possibilities are endless.

The impact of the growth of Google search – and other search engines, though Google quickly dominated the search business, and still does, with more than 90% of the worldwide search market (outside China) – was far broader than it might immediately seem. The direct impact was better access to information, to *more* information and importantly more *useful* information and relevant information. That worked both ways, helping those seeking information and helping those who wanted their information to be found. The less direct but perhaps even more important impact was to take another step along the path began by the invention of the web: making the internet more useful for people with less technical ability and fewer technical skills – not just useful to geeks and nerds but to everyone.

An antisocial network?

The next major development was the growth of social networking and specifically the business model developed by Facebook. Facebook was not the first social network. The UK's *Friends Reunited*, for example, began in 2000, *MySpace* in 2003, while Facebook did not start until

2004. It was, however, the first to develop an effective business model and in doing so established a methodology perhaps even more privacy-invasive than Google's. Mark Zuckerberg understood some key things about how the internet was developing, and found a way to exploit them in an unprecedented way. While sites like Friends Reunited allowed you to find old friends and MySpace gave you a chance to 'show yourself' and your talents, Facebook put that all together and made the *connections* the key. Your 'social network' was all about these connections. Facebook also made it about your ordinary lives and your real world. It made it *personal*.

The business model was the key. Google search was free to those searching; Facebook was free to its members. Friends Reunited had learned the hard way that people expected that: when it decided to ask for even a small fee for membership, it quickly lost almost all of its appeal and heralded its own demise.

Just as for Google, the key was the profiling. Facebook added its own particular slant to this, getting people to profile themselves. Where Google did it surreptitiously, profiling based on what people were searching for, Facebook did most of it openly, persuading people to put in their own personal details, tastes, habits and much more. Facebook worked covertly too: some of the earliest applications on Facebook included quizzes and games where people entered details to see what celebrity they were most like, what their spirit animal might be and so on. They looked like games but the essence was data gathering and self-profiling.

The other key source of data was the *social map*. Who you were 'friends' with. Who you interacted with and how. Who your friends interacted with. What friends you had in common. What all of *their* profiles looked like. What you *liked* – in both the real and the Facebook sense. The levels and richness of this data had immense potential and if at first it was not clear how Facebook would make money, that it *could* make money from it *was* clear. The idea that the data, the profiling, the social maps and all the other connections would be valuable and would enable Facebook to make money was both convincing and a model for others to follow even if the details had yet to be worked out. That in itself had massive implications for privacy as it encouraged more and more data gathering, often speculative. Once the data has been gathered, any business would naturally look for ways to use that data – which again had big implications for privacy.

This did not just mean social networks but pretty much *any* business started to see that the gathering, analysis and use of personal data could be vital. Not just lucrative in itself nor even a competitive advantage, but that a *failure* to engage in this area would put a business at a competitive *disadvantage*. At the same time as the growth of businesses that straddled the online and offline world – most notably Amazon – relied heavily on similar forms of data analysis, essentially *offline* businesses such as Tesco were developing their own data side. Loyalty cards, of which Tesco's Clubcard was perhaps the biggest and best known in the UK, had very close parallels. Data was valuable. Data about people's tastes and behaviour even more so. This together with the rapidly developing techniques of data analysis – the term *big data* was coined in 2005 – meant that the perceived benefits of collection of personal data were immense and created a great incentive for overriding any sense of privacy invasion involved.

Big data and privacy

There is no precise definition of 'big data' but the concept is relatively clear. In essence, it means working with sets of data so big that traditional methods of analysis do not really work but that valuable 'insights' can be gained from analysing them – patterns, trends and unexpected correlations. Big data analysis requires three things: immense volumes of data, computer systems powerful enough to analyse them, and sufficient expertise to programme those systems. All three of these became possible over the same time that the internet developed from a geeky communication system to the all-encompassing network of networks it is today. The belief that 'big data' could be valuable in a wide range of situations grew with similar speed, creating yet another incentive for the gathering of data and imposing further pressures on privacy.

The tensions between big data and privacy have two main dimensions. First, the gathering of data to be incorporated into the data sets is likely in itself to conflict with privacy. Second, the insights that may be gained from the big data analysis may well also amount to privacy invasions. For example, if analysis of shopping habits reveals a link between buying a particular product and holding a particular political view, then using that link to infer an individual's *unspoken* political opinions by looking at their shopping habits would be in effect an invasion of privacy.

Making such links – correlations rather than implying any kind of causation – is very much possible, as has been demonstrated in a whole raft of empirical research. These correlations, importantly, arise from the data rather than from some direct psychological insight. The analysis does not even have to ask why a correlation exists, it just observes that it does. It does not even have to go looking for a particular correlation before finding it – the programmer does not have to ask 'I wonder if people's taste in takeaway food is related to their sexuality' or if whether they follow football correlates with their likelihood of being religious. The nature, richness and structure of data gathered from social media, from searching, from tracking internet browsing and other online behaviour make it ideal for this kind of analysis, while the requirements for it to work – powerful computers and access to those skilled in programming them – make the companies that run internet services particularly suited to performing it.

As well as the privacy issues, there are three important implications of this kind of big data analysis. The first is about neutrality. There is a sense sometimes that big data analysis is somehow 'neutral' – the word 'organic' is even used at times – and the insights and conclusions just emerge from the data, free from bias, prejudice or anything similar. The way that big data analysis works, as noted above, makes it easy for those working with it to believe it, but it is very much *not* the case, both theoretically and in practice, as empirically evidenced.

There are two immediate and mutually reinforceable reasons for this. First, the source data is almost certain not to be neutral or unbiased, from the way it was gathered to the historical and societal biases that exist in the population. Second, those doing the programming, creating the algorithms, are not neutral, even though they may believe they are just letting the data bring the conclusions. There are hidden biases, built-in assumptions about the data, of a wide variety of kinds. There are biases in which data is chosen to be worked on – there is always a choice involved. Applying a biased algorithm to a biased data set, all the while believing that you are neutral and working with a neutral data set, embeds the biases and means that decisions made on the basis of the 'insights' from the analysis are likely to create further biases.

This is particularly relevant to a computer industry dominated by one particular group: rich, white, educated and generally American men. The relatively homogeneous group that were key players in the early days of the internet produced a relatively coherent internet society but not one free from bias. It is a very similar group that dominates what might loosely be called the internet big data industry. The result is that biases are built in, as some high-profile attempts to have beauty contests judged by supposedly neutral 'artificial intelligence' systems have demonstrated. When things like predictive policing are considered, there are even more biases to embed and the results are often even worse.

The second big implication applies more directly to privacy. The nature of big data and the insights derivable from it means that as the amount of data on people as a whole – on the population generally – increases, less data is needed on any particular individual in order to gain an insight into them. In the old, 'small data' world, a great deal of data would be needed to be able to guess something significant such as sexuality, mental health issues or political views. Now it may be possible to have a reasonable guess just on the basis of a handful of data points or even a single piece of information such as a Facebook 'like'. Privacy invasion through big data analysis will become even more of a problem as both the volume of data and the precision of the analysis improve.

The third implication follows directly. In the past, for obvious reasons, certain forms of data have been considered much more important and much more sensitive than others and hence have been given much more protection. This *sensitive* data includes things like political views, sexuality, finance and health. In the big data era, this protection becomes far less effective: if you can derive the most sensitive data from the most mundane everyday data, then any protection would need to cover *all* data, not just the sensitive, and that is far less practical than ever in the current environment. This is a challenge which law has not really addressed and which the technology industry quite naturally does not really want to address. It is nonetheless a challenge that will have to be faced soon.

Government surveillance – the Snowden revelations

Governments have always had their own incentives for gathering information on their citizens – and indeed on others in their states. Some of those motivations are positive. Knowing more about your population can help you to govern better, from knowing more about the state of people's health to better target medical services, or understanding what people are concerned about so as to address those concerns or provide better information and services. Other motivations are driven by need or duty: a government has a duty to keep its people safe, to protect them from crime and to maintain national security. All this requires information and may well involve invading privacy. Some motivations are less positive. Finding political dissidents and suppressing their dissent is perhaps the most obvious but by no means the only reason that a government that leans towards authoritarianism might wish to gather detailed data on the people within its state. Information, as all authoritarians know, is power. The more information that you have, the easier it is to exert that power.

The communications opportunities offered by the internet – including the social opportunities provided by the likes of Facebook – can be used by people who the state would and did view as suspicious and in need of monitoring. Terrorists and criminals use social media, not just because social media can be a tool for organising crimes and acts of terrorism, but because terrorists and criminals are people and almost all people use social media. The logic that suggests appropriately monitoring social media to address serious crime and terrorism, however, can very easily slip into something quite different. When in 2013 the UK government announced that it was monitoring social media postings in order to 'head off' badger cull protests, this was not viewed by those suggesting its having somewhat sinister overtones in relation to legitimate, peaceful protest but as something logical, sensible and appropriate to maintain order.

This is a well-known debate to anyone involved in the study of the role of government surveillance from the pre-internet era – these are familiar ethical dilemmas and balances and generally dealt with through law, codes of practice, systems of oversight and clear regulation. With the growth of the internet, things changed. An opportunity had arisen, and it was hard to resist. Quite how big an opportunity and the extent to which it had been embraced became clear with the revelations of Edward Snowden in the summer of 2013.

What Snowden revealed was not a separate, secret surveillance set-up operated by the spies but a systematic and in-depth infiltration of the *existing* surveillance systems of the businesses that had driven the expansion of the internet. As security expert Bruce Schneier put it: 'The NSA didn't wake up and say, "Let's just spy on everybody." They looked up and said, "Wow, corporations are spying on everybody. Let's get ourselves a copy.'¹ Snowden, who had worked as a contractor for the NSA, revealed a whole range of programmes that the security and intelligence services, not just of the United States but of its allies, were using to put the internet under surveillance.

One of the most direct was *PRISM*, which according to the NSA's own internet documentation provided direct access to the servers of a range of the biggest and most important internet-based companies, including Microsoft, Yahoo!, Google, Facebook and Apple. Snowden revealed a raft of other programmes which effectively piggybacked on the systems of the corporations including *MUSCULAR*, through which the NSA tapped into the then unencrypted traffic between the internal data centres of Google and Yahoo!. They also included programmes which worked independently of the corporations but took advantage of the vast increase in communications that had taken place as a result of the growth of the net – notably *Tempora*, a programme initiated by GCHQ through which it gathered internet traffic data by tapping directly into the fibre-optic cables through which it travelled.

That government agencies were undertaking surveillance on the internet did not really come as a surprise. The scale did, and the way it worked through the normal activities of people on the internet – web browsing, search, social media, entertainment – was what was surprising, though with hindsight it probably should not have been. The lack of public awareness was another matter: it was not just the public that did not know but many politicians, including those whose jobs included the oversight and supervision of the surveillance. That *was* a big deal and brought about some of the biggest reactions to the Snowden revelations, attempting at the very least to get more legal and political control and transparency about the nature and purpose of the surveillance.

The biggest lessons were (or should have been) that we needed to understand that our privacy was being invaded on a systematic basis and not just by corporations but by the authorities. The invention of the web had begun a process that had broadened it from something that was the province of only geeks and nerds to an immense network that played part of almost every aspect of everyone's lives. The development of the business models of first Google and then Facebook had accelerated the process and ensured that privacy invasion and the gathering of personal data had become the norm and a critical part of that growth and broadening. The essence of the model, that is services that are 'free' to the user, making money through the exploitation of those users and their personal data, working through profiling and targeting, had many impacts and many potential uses beyond those envisaged by the businesses that developed them. Among others, governments of all kinds have latched onto the potential that this could provide.

The result is the internet that we have now: all-pervasive, expanding in size and function, unavoidable in almost all societies. It is not just the businesses and governments that have latched onto the potential. From scammers and other criminals to those who wish to manipulate our politics, the applications and implications are distinctly disturbing. This has happened almost without our realising it and to a great extent without our taking appropriate measures either to understand it or deal with the implications. That has to change: we are rapidly reaching the point of no return.

3

what do we know?

Part of the problem with internet privacy is that we don't know everything. Much of what we do know we only discover a significant time after the event. The Snowden revelations in 2013 revealed a set of programmers that had already been in operation for years. The histories of Facebook and Google are littered with examples of egregiously privacy-invasive programmes and ideas being discovered after they have been running for some time just to be abandoned with a little mea culpa from the companies.

We know what we know to a significant extent because of the work of hackers, leakers and investigative journalists – and we also know that there is a great deal that has *not* been hacked or leaked. This also means that the information we have can be incomplete and potentially out of context – and that there is a need for caution about drawing too many conclusions. It should also be remembered that both corporations and governments can sometimes take advantage of this lack of certainty, downplaying the significance of what is happening. It is a difficult balance to find: one interesting aspect of the Snowden revelations was that many of the activities revealed went well beyond what even the more conspiratorial of commentators had speculated about.

What this means is that when looking at what is happening, it is necessary to look also at what *could* be happening. What the technology *enables*. History in this area suggests that if something is possible it is likely. If anything, this kind of speculation underestimates what is going on: the extent to which new and imaginative uses are being found for both technology and data is hard to overestimate. That does not mean engaging in conspiracy theories but rather being prepared and being able to forestall potential problems. With that in mind, this section will look at what we *know* in relation to privacy but also at what this means is *likely* and why.

Having said all that, there is a great deal that we *do* know about how our privacy is being intruded upon and the impact that this has. Some of this has already been covered above from a historical and development perspective. The practical perspective needs to be understood as well. Without going into too many technical details, something both beyond the scope of this book and a bit of a distraction, as new methods are evolving all the time, it should be assumed that almost all actions on the internet *can* be monitored from a technical perspective.

In order to visit a website, for example, you need to send an instruction to the server that website is held on, and the server then needs to send the contents of that website back to you. The instruction will need to include information about where to send the contents – the IP address of the device that you are using – and about the device itself, so that the web page can be sent in an appropriate format. The 'contents' of the web page will include all the links *from* that web page, as well as a whole host of other information. That is just the basics, and both the instructions and the web page are sent through a whole number of other computers, the *network*, all of which have to know some information in order to send the data on its way. At all these points the instructions, web pages and much more can be 'seen' by computers. Some of it needs to be seen, some doesn't, but all has the potential to be seen.

All of this is inevitable by the nature of a network. *How* the information might be intercepted, how the data might be gathered, can vary a lot. 'Cookies', the most familiar way that we are tracked and monitored online, are small pieces of text that a website stores on your computer so that the next time you visit the website it already knows something about your system – from simple things like the operating system you're using to more personal things like whether you've registered with that site, and if so your 'preferences', username, password if you've chosen to let them store it and any options chosen.

You have some control over cookies and after changes in the law in Europe websites are required to ask for your consent before using them.

Cookies can gather information about you and deliver it to the controllers of the relevant website. *Tracking cookies* monitor your web activity often in order to profile your behaviour – and it is not just the controllers of websites that place tracking cookies on your computer, but 'third-party' advertisers and others who work with the controllers of the websites. Sometimes there can be many different cookies that are placed on your computer from a single website, by both the controllers and the third parties. If you use *ad-blocking* software on your browser, as well as blocking the ads it can tell you quite how many cookies are tracking you, which can be distinctly alarming.

Cookies are just one of many ways that we are monitored online. More complex software known as *spyware* is sometimes inserted into your computer, either with your knowledge or consent or without it. Cookies are simple and text-based, basically just recording information; spyware can be much more sophisticated, doing more and learning more about you. Spyware has been used by advertisers, government agencies, cyber criminals and more – the latter also have other methods of data acquisition at their disposal, including the direct hacking of a person's computer, though in practice this is rare enough not to be significant for the vast majority of people.

Browser fingerprinting is somewhat different. Even without cookies a great deal of information can be gathered every time a website is visited, including the details of the computer being used (hardware and software), the kind of browsing software being used and how up to date it is, additional software such as ad-blockers or anti-virus software that has been installed. Much of this is necessary if a website is to be displayed properly on the individual device – particularly given the wide range of devices now used to browse the web, from tiny phones to huge-screened TVs. The level of detail makes it possible in most cases to identify an individual user, without that user logging on to the website and regardless of whether the user allows cookies. One of the key things to understand is that though we can block and monitor cookies and delete them after every browsing session, browser fingerprinting is much harder to prevent.

Another key technique to understand is 'deep packet inspection' ('DPI'). The packet-based nature of internet traffic provides (or at least used to provide) some degree of privacy protection – DPI seeks to break that. As the name suggests, DPI involves an automated inspection of the data packets as they pass through the network – looking inside the envelope, as it were, to see what the data is. It is a more contentious technique than cookies, not just because it is potentially more intrusive but because the act of inspection slows down the traffic, and for the internet for most of its history the speed of data transmission has been critical.

Then there are less 'technical' methods of gathering data. Social media starts with asking people to volunteer information – to self-profile – and continues by persuading people to give more data, to share that data with more people, and by doing so generating even more data about their social maps and interactions. It uses things like the 'like' button, which not only gives information by itself but is deemed to be a kind of act of consent to let the people you 'like' know not just that you've liked them but all kinds of other things about you. All manner of methods are used to cajole people into providing much more information about them, from the relatively direct like quizzes to the less direct like the character creation systems in games which demonstrate things about your own character without you realising it.

Perhaps most importantly there is data that can be *derived* from the data you have provided and has been gathered from you, and from aggregation of that data with other sources of data, both online and offline. That other data may be publicly available, it may be privately acquired through data brokers, and in some cases it may have been hacked, leaked or otherwise illegitimately acquired. This *derived* data includes insights from big data analysis and data effectively 'guessed' by comparing you with people whose profiles show similarities to yours. It should be remembered that in many cases (most, from a commercial perspective) guesswork is entirely acceptable as all that is needed is a reasonable chance of accuracy. For advertising, you don't need that good a 'hit rate' to achieve commercial success.

It should also be remembered that potential harm can come both from when profiling is accurate and from when it is not. An accurate deduction can intrude directly on our privacy, allowing people to know things that we would rather they did not, while an *inaccurate* deduction can mean that inappropriate, unfair or damaging decisions can be made about us. We might be denied credit for unfair reasons, for example, or not be put on a shortlist for a job based on a false presumption. This latter logic is sometimes used to attempt to justify further intrusion into privacy – if more is known, and more accurate information is known, then we can avoid these 'mistakes' – but that just means there is much more likelihood of the first kind of problem, and more interference with our autonomy.

These techniques can be applied not just in relation to *past* data but with *real-time* data, profiling you while you are browsing, playing, watching and everything else that you do. There are other methods of acquiring information of particular and especially intrusive kinds, some increasingly significant. These include location data, biometric data and in particular facial recognition, health data and the data associated with the so-called 'internet of things' – the growing array of 'smart' technology such as smart speakers, camera-connected doorbells and other security systems, internet-linked heating controls and more. These are discussed below, but it is important to understand that this field is expanding all the time and it would be foolish to assume that there are *any* areas in which the internet of things in particular cannot be involved. From 'smart' hairbrushes that monitor hair health and detect split ends to the infamous case of the 'smart' fishtank thermometer through which a casino was hacked in 2017, the range of possibilities is endless.

The next key question is *why* surveillance, data gathering and other privacy intrusions are being performed, and by whom. To understand this, we need to look at the different motivations for intrusions and the different kinds of groups that perform them.

Commercial intrusions

Almost every commercial website gathers personal data on those who visit it. The businesses do it, unsurprisingly, primarily for commercial reasons. Learning about your customers – and about your potential customers – has always been part of doing business, and finding better ways to advertise to them, to *target* advertisements to places and people likely to be receptive to them is also normal practice in business. Analysing markets and customer behaviour in order to develop new services is similarly normal. All of these practices can become easier and more effective in the online environment, particularly with the addition of big data analysis providing new 'insights'.

Some of the reasons that businesses gather and use data about people are therefore obvious, understandable and indeed reasonable, others much more covert and in many ways unreasonable. Profiling a customer on the basis of things that they have done explicitly – for example, their actual purchase records but also things like 'wish lists' or product searches on a business's website – might well seem not just appropriate but to be expected, which matters a great deal in relation to what we feel about our privacy. Profiling them on the basis of the kind of computer they are using to access the website might seem a little less so and yet this is what some companies have done for some time.

In 2012, the travel website *Orbitz* confirmed that it was steering users of Apple Macs to more expensive hotels than those using Windows PCs. It could do this because of three critical elements. First, that the website could identify the kind of device being used to visit it – a minimalist version of *browser fingerprinting*. Second, because Orbitz was able to use this information in coordination with the information that it gathers from what the people actually *do* on the Orbitz website – what hotels they look at, and what hotels they actually book. It was able to identify that people using Macs tended to choose hotels that were significantly more expensive than those chosen by people using Windows PCs, as much as 30% more expensive. Third, it was able to *use* this information to 'tailor' the search results that it gave people when they searched, to suggest more expensive hotels to those searching using Macs, and cheaper ones to those using PCs.

Orbitz did not offer the same hotels at more expensive prices to Mac users, merely pointed them at more expensive hotels, meeting, as Orbitz might have put it, those users' needs and desires more accurately. This does not mean that other commercial operations might not do that – 'tailoring' or 'personalising' prices and services to particular users is technically feasible and in some cases desirable. When it is done covertly – and though Orbitz openly acknowledged the practice in newspaper articles it did not tell the users about it when they were searching – it is far less clear that it is positive, even if it meets the 'needs' of the hotels, Orbitz and the users.

In privacy terms it is intrusive – would most users know or understand that a company would offer something different to them as a result of the particular computer they are using to access their website? The possibilities for similar techniques to be used in ways that produce effects that are far from positive for the users should be fairly obvious. Could you charge someone more if their history suggests they have paid over the odds for products and services before? Would that be ethical – and should it be legal? Perhaps even more perniciously, could you charge someone more for a product that they *need* for health reasons, and need urgently? All of this becomes possible with profiling, targeting and tailoring. Even more concerning, this approach also lies behind some of the political manipulation and targeting of fake news and other forms of misinformation. When you know what people care about and what is likely to persuade them along a path that suits you rather than just them, the opportunities for abuse are substantial.

Another related issue also arises here: one of the key changes from an *offline* world to an online one. When someone goes into a shop in the offline world, they can generally see the prices that the products are sold for – price tags, price lists, catalogues and equivalents. Those prices are the prices for everyone who enters the shop. Everyone is treated equally and fairly. When someone enters a shopping *website* they only see the prices offered *to them*. They do not see the prices that anyone else would get if they entered the same website. They do not know if the prices they are being offered are the same, better or worse than those offered to anyone else.

They do not know if they are being treated fairly – and the algorithmic profiling systems used to determine prices might well be biased in a number of ways. 'Tailored' prices, tailored products, tailored services all sound as though they are positive things, responding to 'customer needs'. Similarly, 'personalisation' sounds as though it is good, but needs to be taken with a distinct pinch of salt, and the techniques and motivations for that personalisation need to be understood. For a company, though it may say that it does all of this for the benefit of the customer, that is likely to be only a small part of the story at best. Businesses exist to make profits – a company has a *duty* to make money for its shareholders – and though the interests of the business and the interests of its customers may well coincide to a great extent, it is the benefit to the business that takes precedence.

The Orbitz example is just an illustration, both of how data can be used and of how that use can involve an intrusion into privacy. It demonstrates one of the most important things to understand about the big data world: the more data is available about a population as a whole, the less data is needed on any particular individual in order to profile them and potentially invade their privacy. It was because Orbitz knew about Mac and PC users as a whole that it felt able to predict the behaviour of individual people on the basis of just the single piece of data that was which kind of computer they were using.

As more data is available, the insights that can be gained can be much deeper and more precise, and without the need for psychological insights or expertise to try to work out *why* an inference might be made. Big data analysis is about correlation rather than causation. From Orbitz's perspective, it did not matter *why* Mac users were more likely to spend more on hotels – it might be that they themselves were more likely to be wealthy, it might be that they were foolish enough to be willing to spend more on style than substance, it might be for all manner of other reasons – it only mattered that they *were* more likely to spend money. Very detailed insights can be gained from the most mundane information if you have sufficient of it. The 2013 study of Facebook 'likes' that was able to link *liking* curly fries to higher intelligence is just one example. Predicting things like sexuality, political view and much more from similarly mundane information has been found to be remarkably accurate.

The three elements in the technique used by Orbitz – gathering data, matching it against insights from existing data, then targeting individuals as a result of that data – form one of the key methods of manipulation of individuals used on the internet. As noted above, the relationship between privacy and autonomy is a close one – privacy is a key protector of autonomy, and intrusions into privacy are often with the view to interference with autonomy.

Manipulation is the essence of most advertising: persuading people to make choices that they might not otherwise make, for example to buy something they would not otherwise buy, or to choose one brand over another. What the internet does, or at least has the potential to do, is make this more effective and more direct. It is not something exactly new, but that does not mean that it is not something that should cause concern. Very much the reverse: the potential magnification that the internet provides to these old techniques means that it needs to be taken much more seriously. In the 1950s and 1960s there were fears about 'subliminal' advertising – there are still laws against it, even though at the time the effectiveness seems to have been much overblown and perhaps false.

What is happening now – and what has the potential to happen in the future – could make those fears something real.

Masters of manipulation?

It should not be a surprise that an internet whose business models are primarily built around advertising – both Google and Facebook revenues are primarily from advertising – is one in which manipulation is baked in. The infrastructure allows it and the business models actively encourage it. It is in the interests of Google and Facebook and those who use similar business models not just to be able to manipulate people but to be able to prove that they can manipulate people. In the old environment this was not really possible: you pay for an advertising slot on TV or a place on a newspaper page with an assumption or even a hope that by getting an audience you will get attention. Online, this can now be *proven* by whether people actually click on the ads. A great deal of online advertising relies on this: it is 'pay per click' so if the ads don't get clicked the advertiser doesn't pay.

Google and Facebook go much further than this. Google Analytics, for example, provides very detailed information about the traffic on your site, including advertising effectiveness. Facebook has tried to take this demonstration of effectiveness to another level, funding and supporting research into many different aspects of the way it works – proving the effectiveness of its manipulative capabilities, though it would not present it in this way. One notorious example of this research was its 2014 'emotional contagion' experiment. Facebook demonstrated to a statistically significant degree that it could manipulate the emotions of its users by algorithmically altering their timelines.

The experiment involved nearly 700,000 people – that these people were not informed that their emotions were being played with was interesting from an ethical perspective but rather revealing in terms of how Facebook operates. These people were divided into three groups. For one group, postings that an algorithmic 'sentiment analysis' suggested were 'happy' were given more prominence, while postings that seemed to be sad were demoted. For the second group, the reverse: happy postings demoted, sad ones promoted. For the third group, both happy and sad postings were demoted, and emotionally neutral postings given more prominence.

The results were revealing. The group given a happier timeline became measurably happier – as assessed by another algorithmic sentiment analysis of the postings of those users. The group given a sadder timeline became measurably sadder. The third group, those given a more emotionally neutral timeline, produced perhaps the most interesting but the least publicised results: they engaged less with Facebook. So not only did the experiment reveal the possibilities of manipulating users' emotions, but also Facebook had an *incentive* to make more emotional content have more prominence. This, as shall be seen, matters significantly in relation to things like political polarisation and the spread of fake news and other forms of misinformation.

When this is combined with other elements of Facebook's experimentation, the potential impact becomes even more significant. Facebook has been able to demonstrate that it can improve voter turnout and influence people into registering to vote. Further, it showed that *personalised* messages were one of the more effective methods – being told that your friends had voted in particular. Though this may all seem positive – indeed, Mark Zuckerberg has referred to it in his responses to criticism about Facebook's role in democracy – when more factors are brought into play the positivity is more questionable.

One of these is Facebook's use of 'racial affinity' groups. While targeting by race – racial profiling – is not explicit on Facebook, and in various places would be considered illegal, Facebook has what amounts to a way around it. Facebook does not target by race per se, but by the race that you show 'affinity' towards, from a cultural perspective. This makes it seem to be about 'tastes' rather than race. A particularly graphic example of this came with the marketing for the film *Straight Outta Compton*, about rappers NWA. Three different trailers were produced, and delivered to different 'segments of the market'. For those showing 'affinity' to African Americans, the trailer assumed knowledge of NWA and their background. For those showing affinity to white Americans, more background was provided. For Hispanics, Spanish subtitles were provided.

All of this – the emotional contagion, the voter registration, the actual voting, the racial profiling and targeting – can combine together to produce targeted political effects: make those likely to be your political allies happier; encourage them to participate more in the political process. For your enemies, the reverse: make them sadder; discourage them from voting or make them less trusting. It is not just racial profiling that can be done but profiling on the basis of politics, sexuality, religion, disability and much more. As we put almost all aspects of our lives online in one way or another, we become especially vulnerable to this kind of profiling and influence. When the biases built into algorithmic systems are added to the equation this makes it even worse. And, of course, all of this is based on the privacy-invasive techniques of data gathering, profiling and targeting. The privacy aspect is the key: the invasion of privacy is crucial for the manipulation to be done, both in the gathering of the data in order to perform the profiling and then in enabling the targeting that allows the manipulation to happen.

Tailoring and 'personalisation' are not limited to Facebook but have been part of the way that the internet works for over a decade. Google has been 'personalising' search results by default since 2009 – and what Google puts at the top of search results determines to a great extent what links are followed. Even the search results themselves can have a huge impact on people – how often do people just read the headlines and snippets of the pages in their search results rather than go to the actual page? Amazon's recommendations have been personalised since 2010. This model has to all intents and purposes become the norm on the internet, based on the use of personal information with the intention to 'influence' or 'persuade'. What works in relation to searching for information or for finding products to buy will also work for things like news and politics – imagining that this does not really matter because it is only advertising and so does no real *harm* is to miss the point.

This kind of targeting and manipulation is only one of the reasons and one of the ways that businesses intrude into our privacy. There are businesses that track or monitor us purely to gather data – both in general terms, to gather background data that as noted before makes it easier to gather insights from individuals, and to gather specific data about particular individuals or types of individuals, for potential future use or sale. There are those who aggregate and analyse this data, using big data techniques to gain insights from the data that could have commercial value. There are the 'pure' advertisers – not attached to search or social networking but who monitor people in order to be able to target advertisements on their own.

Then there are things like price comparison websites or credit checking websites that offer apparently free services but while doing so gather data directly – you provide highly granular data that has great potential use and give them permission to analyse and aggregate that data, in return for their 'checking' your data with existing data elsewhere, and generating further data for themselves. There are 'review' sites for products and services – and for hotels, cities, beaches, etc. – that also provide 'free' services and at the same time gather masses of data both private and otherwise. Again, it must be remembered that by gathering more data *in general*, it becomes possible to learn more about specific individuals from less data. If a travel service, for example, has detailed information about the profiles of people who visit a particular place, then it becomes easier for the service to profile you when *you* visit that particular place.

Special kinds of data – and special kinds of data gathering

So far, the arguments in this section have focused on the most direct and basic of data that arises through our actions on the internet: which websites we visit, what we search for, who we contact and why, what information we provide about ourselves and of course the data that can be derived from all of this data. This can provide those who wish to profile, target, influence and manipulate us with a great deal of information and a wide range of opportunities. As the internet and the *uses* of the internet have developed, there are certain particular kinds of data and methods of data gathering that have a particular significance and are worthy of special attention.

Location data

There are a number of reasons that location data has become one of the most important areas. It provides a link between the 'real' and the online worlds, both allowing a direct connection to be made with the individual in the 'real' world and making any data gathered about their online activities potentially more valuable. It can also 'verify' in some ways the online behaviour – if you know someone is searching online for information about a place and at the same time is actually in or around that place, that strengthens the connection.

If they're searching for restaurants, for example, it might mean they're really going to eat. If they're looking for job opportunities, they might be a genuine candidate. Location data also helps establish patterns:

working out where someone lives, where they work, where they shop and socialise is relatively easy if you can follow their movements. Finally, and most importantly, location data is both easy to gather and easy to analyse. As we have shifted towards using mobile devices to connect to the internet – primarily phones, but also tablets, smart watches, sat-nav devices and connected cars, GPS-connected and app-controlled hireable electric bikes and scooters, and much more – that location data can be and generally is collected automatically and in a usable form.

Though mobile phones give you the option to turn off location services, there are a vast array of apps, including some of the most used, that either require them to be turned on or only provide full functionality when they are turned on. Even without location services enabled, it is possible to gather location data from mobiles through their cell connection. When people use the various mapping apps, this not only gives their current location but can establish plans, interests and activities. Massively popular ride-hailing apps like Uber and Lyft provide yet more location data in the same way, of both riders and drivers, while the various transport 'smart cards' (or smartphones) that you 'check in' with gather similar data for public transport. Smartphones themselves bring all of this together.

Location data is one of the key ways to make the link between the 'online' person and their physical presence. If you can use it to identify their home, you can work with other data (e.g. electoral rolls, property registers, club membership data, etc.) to identify the precise individual. If gathered in real time, location data allows authorities to arrest people immediately – or stop them joining protest marches and meetings. The potential for misuse of location data is significant.

Another key aspect to location data is that it reveals not only where you are, but where you are not. If you are supposed to be at work and your location data reveals that you are not, an employer might want to know – and again, the possibilities of abuse of this kind of information are significant. In 2010, privacy advocates from the Netherlands used a website called *pleaserobme.com* to demonstrate one of the key possibilities. Using publicly available data primarily from social media and the 'check-in' site *Foursquare*, pleaserobme.com was able to discover (a) where people lived and (b) that they were not at home. It then posted a picture of their home, also publicly available, and their name, saying 'please rob me, I'm not home'. All of this was done in real time and using publicly available information.

The website developers made it clear that this was not intended as a tool for burglary but as a demonstration of the foolishness of making this kind of information available, but although this was back in 2010 there is little sign that people are becoming any less reticent in sharing this kind of data. Changing these kinds of habits is one of the keys to dealing with our privacy problems.

Though pleaserobme.com used information people had willingly provided, these days much location data is provided automatically and without those providing it realising that they are doing so. 'Location stamps' in the metadata of photographs posted to social media are just one example. Many apps ask for location data to be turned on in order to function at all and many users will just click OK to everything when they install the apps. This means that location services are on whenever they use the app, even in the background. For many more, location services are just left on all the time for convenience. As mobile access to the internet has become the norm this has enormous significance.

Health data

Health data is some of the most sensitive forms of all. Confidentiality is the cornerstone of the relationship between doctor and patient – and people are very sensitive about revealing any health conditions to others. On the other side, health data has the potential to be both exceptionally useful in finding ways to treat illnesses and exceptionally lucrative given the amount of money spent in the medical market.

There are subsets of health data that do not fit into the 'medical' market quite so directly: fitness data, dieting data and things like monitoring menstruation. All this is also highly valuable and can be monitored and either recorded by devices or input manually. Health data is extremely suitable for big data analysis and for the expanding areas of artificial intelligence and machine learning. This quite naturally creates tensions but, as is common throughout the data privacy area, it is generally the privacy that gives way – but not always. Feelings about health data have sometimes been so strong as to mean that privacy has in effect 'won', at least in the short term.

Health data can be derived from a number of sources. First, there is direct data gathered by doctors – patient records including symptoms, measurements, prescriptions. etc. In the UK this data is held by individual

GP practices and by hospitals (and in particular NHS trusts). Researchers from academia, government bodies, the pharmaceutical industry, the insurance industry and others negotiate with those GP practices and hospitals to get access to this data.

Next, there is the data gathered through monitoring people's searching and browsing history. People search so regularly for symptoms and treatments that Google has claimed to be able to monitor public health even better, at times, than the doctors, most notably with its 'Google Flu Trends' system which in 2009 claimed to be able to predict flu outbreaks in the United States nearly as well as the official Centers for Disease Control. That claim was challenged and ultimately in effect debunked in terms of accuracy and speed, but even so the predictive ability of analysis of search data remains significant and potentially lucrative for those selling treatments for flu and other diseases.

Another key and growing source of health data is the expanding market for 'wearable' fitness devices – Fitbits, smart watches (most notably the Apple Watch) and their equivalents. These can monitor your pulse, activity, sleep, blood pressure, weight and much more, and make inferences from them in terms of both fitness and health. They work, like other 'smart' devices, through connection to the internet and the transmission of their wearers' health data into a central server for analysis.

One of the most (in)famous projects in this area in the UK was Google's 'DeepMind' AI subsidiary's project with the Royal Free Hospital in London. This used smartphone apps to monitor kidney patients' conditions, gathering detailed health data not only to deal with life-threatening conditions in real time, but also for long-term research into those conditions. The boundaries between the functions are blurred, as is the picture of who really benefits from all of this: individual patients, the Royal Free, Google or the public. The Royal Free ended up being castigated by the Information Commissioner's Office for its misuse of patient data, including a failure to inform the patients properly about how their data would be used.

That was one of the critical factors in one of the biggest data project failures in the health field: the *care.data* farrago. This massive project organised by NHS England aimed to pull together patient records from all the GP practices in England into a single database, for access by researchers. The system was intended to be 'opt-out' so that unless people actively objected their data records would be added to the database. Information about the project was supposed to be sent to all the households in England, telling them about the project, which was supposed to mean that they 'consented' to their data being included.

The project ran into problems from the start, indicative of the privacy issues surrounding such sensitive data as health data. The information provided was poorly put together, not explaining how to opt out properly among other things. GPs were not properly informed either – so when patients went to GPs to ask about it, the GPs often did not even know about the project, let alone have answers to any questions.

It was also far from clear who the 'researchers' who would have access to the data would be – and those behind the project did not seem to understand that people would care about that. Many people would be happy for their data to be used by universities to find new cures or treatments for their diseases but would be unhappy to help big pharmaceutical companies make more money or insurance companies find ways to deny people coverage or increase premiums.

GPs were unhappy that patients might not trust them enough to talk to them if they feared that their records could be accessed by others that they *did not* trust. That may have been the decisive factor: many GPs opted out themselves and said that they would advise their patients to do the same. The whole project quickly gained a very bad reputation – and was scrapped even before it came into action, causing a great embarrassment to the NHS, wasting a good deal of money, and losing the potential research benefits, primarily as a result of a failure to take privacy and confidentiality into account.

The care.data saga demonstrated how much people cared about their data, but it has not really slowed down the growth of the health data field. The UK may be a special case in terms of health data as the attitude to public (the NHS) rather than private health provision is a factor that is either absent or much less important than in other states. In the United States in particular, the situation is very different and it is the United States that drives the development of the technologies that are involved in the gathering and processing of health data.

Facial recognition data – and other biometrics

Biometrics refers to making recordings, measurements and calculations of physical, behavioural or related characteristics of people, suitable for digitisation and analysis, and used primarily for identification. Examples include fingerprints, retinal scans and voice recognition, but the most commonly known and perhaps the most important at the current stage of the internet is *facial recognition*. This is the analysis of photographs that include faces in order to identify the individuals pictured – and it has become increasingly common in a vast range of internet contexts.

It can be used as a verifier of identity – to unlock phones via things like Apple's 'FaceID', to access services and more – which is more convenient and reliable than using passwords. Facebook is of course very keen on facial recognition, among other things using it to 'tag' people in photographs, enriching its social maps and verifying the strengths of relationships that they know exist online. If two people are in photographs together, rather than just communicating online, they have a qualitatively different relationship. Facial recognition data can link with location data: metadata embedded in photographs that records where they were taken, or recognisable buildings or landscapes that can be algorithmically identified and matched with their locations. With the vast number of photographs being put online, a consequence of the almost universal take-up of internet-linked camera-equipped smartphones, the opportunities and applications for facial recognition have blossomed.

Facial recognition is another way to link online and offline identities, which as noted throughout this book is one of the keys to serious privacy invasion. It can also be used to link one set of data to another – images captured by CCTV, for example, with images on social media, with images retained by government for passport or visa applications or at border checks. The benefits for the security services of being able to do this are clear – but so are the potential misuses and abuses.

Behavioural biometric indicators are less obvious but may become even more significant in certain contexts. They include typing patterns – we each have our own patterns, how long we take to move from one letter to another, even the pressure we put on each letter – and related to that the physical patterns of our mouse, trackpad or phone screen use. Even how we hold our phones and walk with them: as modern phones have highly sensitive motion sensors and pressure-sensitive screens, all this can be used to identify us whether we want to be identified or not. Much of it is gathered by our devices automatically, whether for security purposes or 'recognition' for predictive purposes or some way of improving efficiency or future product development. This can become a kind of 'browser fingerprinting' on steroids: identifying individuals pretty much whatever precautions they take to protect their identity.

The very thing that makes biometric data so useful for security systems is what makes it so potentially vulnerable and privacy invasive. We can change passwords when they are compromised but we can't change our biometrics. Once our biometrics have been captured, whoever has access to them has a degree of control over us that is nigh on impossible to remove. That is especially true in relation to what is in one way the ultimate form of biometric data – DNA. This is something that is being increasingly collected – again in a number of different ways and for seemingly very different purposes.

Law enforcement agencies use it in investigations. It is used in medicine, both for individual use and for research in an increasing number of areas. It is also used for establishing familial links, ancestry and ethnic heritage both for specific uses such as establishing paternity and for the growing field of historical and related research. Commercial operators like the direct DNA service *23andMe* and more general genealogical sites such as *ancestry.com* do the same. Ancestry.com includes a button saying 'Take a DNA test and uncover your origins'.

23andMe has on its front page the message 'Your genes have a lot to say about your health, traits and ancestry', which makes the key point. DNA can be used to derive an enormous amount of other data, from familial links to information about health – as well as being a near-perfect identifier of individuals.

These are both its strengths and its vulnerabilities – and why protecting what happens to DNA data is critical for privacy, and people's apparent willingness to hand it over just to discover something that might be interesting about their past and origins is not at all advisable. It is another area where giving up our own privacy has a potential impact on others' privacy: anyone with familial links will share certain aspects of DNA, and may be identified through that sharing. The information that may be ascertained from your DNA in the future is potentially far greater than what we know now, so the privacy impact of handing over DNA *now* is also far greater.

The internet of things

The term 'internet of things' is, like many in this field, somewhat vague. Broadly, it refers to physical 'things' that are linked to the internet, controlled through the internet, or are able to communicate with other 'things' through the internet. Common examples include voice-controlled 'smart speakers' through which music and other content can be streamed from the net, camera-equipped doorbells that can show you who's knocking at your door wherever you are, heating systems remotely controlled through apps on your smartphone, 'smart' televisions and so on.

Almost anything can be connected to the internet and many things that it still seems almost unimaginable *have* been connected to the internet – the 'smart' hairbrush that detects things like split ends as it brushes is far from the most unusual. There are smart cat-flaps that alert us when our cats come and go, smart forks that make noises to cover up our slurps, smart umbrellas that tweet us if it's going to rain and more.

Internet of things devices have a number of common features. All communicate with some kind of a server, most sending data gathered through sensors of various sorts – microphones, cameras, thermometers, movement sensors, pressure sensors and many others – or received from other connected devices. That data is then used to do various things, subjected to aggregation and analysis in what amounts to some kind of big data fashion. For example, as well as sending you, the songs you ask for, your smart speaker will gather data about what you listen to and when, using that to profile you and people like you, and build up a record of your voice commands, while your smart hairbrush will gather information not only about your hair through its various sensors, but also about how you brush, when you brush and so on – again building a profile which is then analysed along with the profiles of everyone else who uses those brushes.

Internet of things devices challenge privacy in at least two significant ways. The first is through the various sensors, many of which have to be always on. Voice-activated devices will have microphones that are always on if they are to be 'turned on' by a request. Camera-equipped systems may also always be on – or may be activated more often than the users realise. That has an obvious privacy impact – installing a voice-activated smart speaker means installing a permanent listening device in your living room, for example. The second privacy impact is through the data. Not only are you installing a sensor system, but also you are installing a self-profiling system and allowing your profile to be used for the benefit of those from whom you have acquired your smart device.

The internet of things also generates location data: as each device has a physical existence it has a physical location. Often, that physical location is key to how the device works: doorbells, heating systems, cars, etc. There is a whole class of internet of things devices that work directly with health data: the various wearables such as Fitbits. For some devices it is both health and location data with all the issues discussed above.

Internet of things devices add an extra level of vulnerability, particularly as they are often built with less security than more traditional computer devices, to keep the prices low enough for the 'leisure' market. A cheap webcam won't have the security of an expensive laptop, and the more 'novelty' items – 'smart' toys, for example – barely have any security at all. This makes them eminently hackable as they are necessarily connected to the internet and generally controlled through the internet. If you can control them, so can others. Some very notable hacks have happened through hackers gaining control of massive numbers of internet of things devices and using those devices to send data to overload targeted servers elsewhere on the internet. In 2016, for example, a hack of webcams was used to take down Netflix, Google, Spotify and Twitter for most of the United States.

This vulnerability also creates another layer of privacy issues. Hacking a connected device can make available the data of all the devices on not only the immediate network around that device – your 'smart' kettle being used as a route into all the devices in your home – but potentially other networks too. Someone else's smart heating system could be used to reach into the server that their heating provider uses in order to locate and hack *any* of the heating systems using the same provider – and thus access the relevant home networks, including the laptops and phones, on the same WiFi router. Find the weakest point on a network – the person who doesn't change their password, or uses an easily guessed password, or the same password on all their devices – and the rest of the network can become vulnerable along with all the data on it. This kind of vulnerability exists in many forms across the internet but the internet of things makes it especially likely, and the hackers know this.

The interaction of different 'smart' devices with each other creates further profiling and derived data without people involved having either control or understanding of it. Many devices and the systems behind them are provided by the internet giants, Google and Amazon in particular but

Apple and increasingly Facebook, tightening and deepening their profiling and control.

For these reasons the internet of things is an area distrusted by many in the technology field. They know that smart meters can become tools for profiling behaviour through energy use and smart cities become surveillance cities – something not lost on the 2019 protestors in Hong Kong, who took special precautions to try to avoid being tracked (e.g. wearing scarves to cover their faces to avoid facial recognition and using cash rather than 'smart cards' for public transport) as well as trying to destroy 'smart' lampposts that they knew were recording their movements and activities.

Political data – and political manipulation

A final special category of data is what might loosely be called 'political' data: data about people's political interests, views, history, connections and beliefs. Some of this is direct – party membership, any official political activities such as candidacy for office or donations to parties – but much more of it is less direct, including political postings on social media, 'likes' and 'favouriting' of political stories and events. Even more is entirely indirect: political preferences and beliefs *derived* from other data, for example through big data analysis. Unsurprisingly, this data is both very sensitive and very sought after: the possibility of using the data for political purposes has become increasingly clear and the exploitation of it has been one of the most notable expansion areas in recent years.

Political parties have grasped the usefulness of data with both hands. They use a variety of techniques, some overt and consensual, consulting with their members and supporters, some much more insidious, including things like discovering how many people on the electoral role share your name and signing a petition against female genital mutilation, which were in effect data gathering exercises with their real nature obscured or revealed only in the small print or un-clicked-on terms and conditions. All the main parties have used these kinds of tactics, which stretch data protection law at the very least. For this and related reasons, the Information Commissioner's Office undertook an investigation into data and political campaigning in 2017–2018, taking action in a number of cases, noting that '[o]ur investigation uncovered significant issues, negligence and contraventions of the law'. The main takeaway from the report was that the whole situation is confused and confusing to regulators, political parties, and most importantly to voters.

One critical area where this plays out is social media. Parties, pressure groups and others not only engage directly on Facebook, Twitter and other social media, but also establish close relationships with social media companies. In the United States in particular those relationships are very much encouraged by the social media companies and others in the internet world. Empirical research into the role of Facebook, Twitter, Google and Microsoft in the 2016 presidential election showed active collaboration between staff at the companies and in the political campaigns. The researchers noted that 'technology firms are motivated to work in the political space for marketing, advertising revenue, and relationship-building in the service of lobbying efforts' and that 'representatives at these firms serve as quasi-digital consultants to campaigns, shaping digital strategy, content, and execution' (Kreiss and McGregor, 2018). There are advantages to both the firms and the political campaigns of this kind of collaboration but potentially very significant implications to people's autonomy and the integrity of the political process.

The key is to understand that what happens in the commercial world, with commercial invasions of privacy and commercial use of profiling and targeting in order to influence behaviour, can and does happen in the same way with politics. The techniques are the same: it is only the parameters that change. A huge amount of our political action now takes place online, from access to political information via online news sources to political discussion on the various forums of social media, to our interactions with politicians. MPs engage with their constituents via Facebook and Twitter, parties put out their political broadcasts and post their manifestos online. Political journalists seem to spend all their time on Twitter. Posts, pictures, memes, videos, coverage and live commentary of events all happen online and all are shared by 'influencers' on social media.

All the techniques and problems that exist for commercial activity can therefore be applied – the profiling, targeting and influencing. Fake news and other forms of misinformation are based on these kinds of techniques. Content can be tailored to be persuasive – choosing topics that profiling suggests will persuade – and targeted at those likely to be persuaded. Just as for commercial advertising, this is about nudging people in directions they are already predisposed to go. It is not about converting someone from being a Labour voter to a Tory but about making a Labour supporter a little less enthusiastic, less likely to be bothered to go out and vote, less likely to persuade their friends to vote, or making a Tory supporter *more* likely to vote and actively campaign. It is about seeding information in places where it is likely to be extensively shared among networks to spread the information to exactly those likely to be influenced in an electoral context. It is about creating false accounts – either human or automated – that will enable that sharing and boost numbers in what amounts to *astroturfing*, a term coined by Lloyd Bentsen in the 1980s, which means the creation of a fake 'grassroots' movement. AstroTurf is fake grass, so astroturfing is a fake grassroots movement.

This kind of operation is what lay behind the Facebook/Cambridge Analytica affair. This should not be seen as a rogue event, a misuse of the system, so much as a logical use of an infrastructure designed for manipulation. All the techniques used are following patterns used for advertising, from the creation of attractive content that meets the tastes and desires of potential customers, to the profiling and then targeting of those potential customers.

Tailoring and personalisation, seen as primarily positive things for advertising, become rather less so when applied in the political realm. Further, this is not just about advertising but about all kinds of content – stories that reinforce opinions, whether false or true, for example – and not just about obviously political actors or content. Big data analysis can provide the 'insights' that allow manipulation in indirect and far from obvious ways. It is the profiling and targeting that matter, not the specific contents, and the underlying key is a failure to respect privacy.

Governments and internet privacy

The actions of governments in relation to the internet are multifaceted. There is a political aspect, of course, and many of the issues discussed in the previous section apply directly to governments in power. There are more prosaic areas too – the provision of government information and government services at every level, from bin-collection times to taxation, all of which allow and encourage data collection that is beneficial for all.

The better information about the population that a government has, the better it can understand the needs of that population and the better it can target and satisfy those needs. This applies in all fields, from public health to transport, from education to the environment. There are classical privacy slippery slopes here: the more information that is gathered, the more potential intrusion on privacy, and the more information is gathered, the more temptation there can be to use that information. Nowhere is this more evident than in the fields of law enforcement, public order and national security, which is where the role of government surveillance comes into play.

The UK government's reaction to the 2013 Snowden revelations was very different from the US reaction. Where there was a lot of hand-wringing, angry questioning and heart-searching in the United States – and even the reining back of some surveillance programmes – the UK government began by essentially saying 'of course we're doing this kind of thing, and we're doing it for good reasons'. When their actions were challenged in the courts as not having a legal basis, the intelligence and security services reacted by providing more information, including acknowledgement of what they were doing and why, and codes of conduct for those doing them – which meant that though their activities *had* been unlawful, those same activities were *now* legitimate.

Taking this a stage further, the Home Office planned and executed a change in the law. To replace the old opaque, convoluted legal justification which effectively shoe-horned the actions into laws created for very different purposes, it brought in the Investigatory Powers Act 2016 ('IPA'), which set out in detail what the authorities would be able to do. This both explained and justified some extreme levels of intrusion. The authorities judged, correctly as it turned out, that people would support them and that privacy advocates, though they succeeded in labelling the IPA a 'snooper's charter' in the public debate at least, would not be able to win the political arguments against that intrusion.

As a result of this, the IPA is quite revealing about the activities that governments use in their surveillance. It sets out the powers that the police, intelligence and security services, and others can use: interception of communications (covering the content of communications), acquisition and retention of communications data (data surrounding the communications – metadata), and 'equipment interference' (effectively hacking into computer systems in order to gather data) as the main types of surveillance. Communications, in these terms, include all kinds of things that people might not traditionally consider 'messages' – anything you 'send' to a server, such as an instruction to visit a website, a click on a web page and much more.

The IPA also enables 'bulk powers': using any of the aforesaid powers but at a bulk level, where the scale of 'bulk' is effectively unlimited. In addition, the IPA can be used to acquire 'bulk personal data sets': loosely defined but essentially the right to acquire any set of personal data, from a hospital's medical records or a company's customer database to pretty much anything else. The IPA also sets out the concept of an 'internet connection record', intended to be like an 'itemised phone bill for the internet' that communications providers could be expected to create. Such a thing is not really possible in most circumstances and to ask for it betrays a fundamental misunderstanding of the way the internet works, but the intention is clear: to be able to keep a record of everyone's activities on the internet.

One further set of powers is also granted by the IPA and other earlier surveillance laws: the power to compel people and indeed communications providers to breach their own privacy protections, from handing over passwords to the potential inclusion of 'back doors' to give the authorities access to communications. Though the desire to undermine or reduce the effectiveness of countermeasures to surveillance is understandable, the effect is potentially disastrous, undermining security itself. The campaigns against end-to-end encryption – where the encryption is applied at the sender's end and only reversible at the receiver's end, so that even the communication provider cannot read the message or help the authorities read the message – that many governments engage in is shameful.

These powers, as can be seen, are extensive and intended in effect to be exhaustive – to make it possible to put all activity on the internet under surveillance, and to acquire any data about anyone on the internet. It also reveals the interaction between government and commercial surveillance: these powers are all about tapping into commercial activities and commercial databases. Equipment interference would include things like piggybacking on tracking systems created by advertisers, using cookies, spyware or other software following the same lines as those designed by advertisers.

One of the key questions about internet privacy, whether to be more concerned about commercial or government surveillance, is thus relatively easily answered: the two cannot easily be separated and we should be concerned about both. In most situations, it can be assumed that if commerce is putting us under surveillance, governments will be able to tap into that surveillance too.

Government surveillance, however, has something of a different impact to corporate surveillance. The police can arrest us and lock us up – or even, in some places, kill us – and this monopoly of (legal) force is rightfully concerning. Surveillance is part of an overall power relationship between the government and the governed and should be seen in that context. It has two dimensions:

- *Overt* surveillance has a chilling and control effect: the 'Panopticon' effect, named after a concept for a prison suggested by Jeremy Bentham. The Panopticon was a circular prison with a guardhouse at the centre and all the cells visible from that centre. The idea was that the prisoners knew that at any moment they could be watched by the guards – and that knowing this would make them behave better. The logic applies to whole societies: if you know that you are under government surveillance, you might be less likely to behave 'badly' in the terms that the government would see it. Highly surveilled societies encourage conformity: the evidence from East Germany under the Stasi is perhaps the best example.
- *Covert* surveillance, on the other hand, has a 'power effect': in essence, knowing more about someone, or being able to monitor their movements and actions, gives you power over them. If a government knows where a dissident group is going to meet, it can send agents to arrest them. If they monitor a terrorist's communications, they can find out their fellow conspirators, allies and funders.

The difference between the effects of overt and covert surveillance mean that they are used differently by authorities. Sometimes authorities want to exaggerate their surveillance systems so that people curb their behaviour even when the authorities couldn't really stop them. Sometimes they underplay their surveillance so that people they want to monitor do not take countermeasures or change tactics. These two factors mean that we can rarely be sure that what we are told about government surveillance is giving us the real picture.

Scammers, hackers and other criminals

For those operating outside or at least on the borders of legality, pretty much all the tools and techniques used by others are available, shorn of any legal or ethical restrictions. They can and do use privacy invasion to profile and target their victims, or to acquire key information to use for identity theft and related frauds. They can and do use big data analysis to identify potential routes to scamming and worse. They can and do acquire data from other sources – hacking, buying or otherwise acquiring data through the less scrupulous areas of the internet.

If a back door is created for law enforcement agencies, or a weakness in any system is identified and not immediately addressed, they can and will use those back doors or exploit those weaknesses. They use cookies to track people, spyware to watch their activities and so on. If a new technique or a new technology is developed for lawful purposes there will be people looking for how it can be used for criminal purposes: this pattern has been observed through the history of the internet and privacy-invasive techniques are no exception.

In addition, there are specific techniques developed for criminal purposes: phishing and click-jacking are just two of them. Phishing is asking people to give their personal information – often login names and passwords – by pretending to be someone else. Sending an email pretending to be from your bank, for example, or setting up a website that looks like an official one, with a login box that actually sends your details to the criminals. Click-jacking is even more insidious. A 'transparent' button is created as part of an overlay to a website, placed where another button already exists. When you click where you think the other button is, you actually click the transparent button, activating something that the criminal has set up – often again sending your details to the criminals, or installing some piece of spyware or similar on your computer.

There are other techniques being developed all the time, often taking advantage of 'normal' user behaviour, and either mimic or hijack 'normal' websites or internet services. They exploit our tendency not to take privacy seriously – and of the general lack of privacy protection on the internet.

Privacy protections

So far, the focus has been on the challenges to privacy on the internet and their implications, but it is important to understand that there are ways in which these challenges are at least partially addressed, ways that our privacy can be (and to an extent in practice is) protected. Privacy is considered to be a human right and human rights are given legal protection.

In relation to internet privacy, that legal protection comes in two main categories: first, the direct protection of privacy and in particular privacy of data and communications; second, in the limitations and controls over legal invasions of privacy, for example in the oversight and accountability built into government surveillance law. There is also some specific criminal law that applies directly to the internet and in particular privacy: in the UK, the *Computer Misuse Act* covers things like hacking and other forms of illegal access to computers and data.

Probably the most important of these is *data protection* law. Data protection is intended to give people some degree of control over how data about them is treated – how it is gathered, processed, held or transferred. The heart of data protection law is the concept of *personal data*. This is an intentionally broad concept. As the Information Commissioner's Office (ICO), which administers data protection law in the UK, describes it, 'Personal data is information that relates to an identified or identifiable individual'. This means *any* data that is linked or can be linked to an individual. It does not have to be important data, intimate data, significant data or anything special and it does not have to be actually linked to the individual, but if it *can* be linked to the individual that is enough. In a data-rich and data-driven environment like the internet this covers a vast range of data.

Data protection law is European in origin. In the internet era, it has been governed first by the Data Protection Directive from 1995 (backed up by the more specialised 'ePrivacy Directive' covering electronic communications in particular) and more recently by the General Data Protection Regulation (GDPR), which was finalised in 2016 and came into force in 2018. The basic ideas of both are the same: the biggest real differences with the GDPR relate to enforcement and punishment (massively increasing fines for those breaking the law) and 'reach' (the GDPR explicitly sets out to be enforceable on any company anywhere in the world that aims its services at people in the EU). The data protection principles are relatively straightforward. As set out in the GDPR:

1. Data must be processed 'lawfully, fairly and transparently'

2. Data must be 'collected for specified, explicit and legitimate purposes and not further processed in a manner that is incompatible with those purposes' – purpose limitation

3. Only the data necessary for a task should be collected – 'data minimisation'
4. Data must be accurate – and reasonable checks need to be made to ensure this accuracy
5. Data must only be held as long as it is needed – storage limitation
6. Data must be kept securely and confidentially
7. Those who control and process data can be held accountable for that data and the processing.

Quite how these principles apply to the kind of things that happen on the internet is more complex: each of the principles is subject to a great deal of discussion and dispute. For example, what constitutes lawful processing and the 'legitimate' purposes for data collection and processing is often very hard to pin down. With social media, for example, what exactly is the purpose that any data is gathered? Has it been specified explicitly? Do people even know how their data is used? The GDPR set out a number of possible 'lawful bases' for processing data:

1. Consent
2. Fulfilment of a contract
3. Satisfying a legal obligation
4. The 'vital interests' of the data subject (e.g. keeping them alive)
5. Performing a task in the public interest (mostly by authorities or those working for authorities)
6. The 'legitimate interests' of either the processor or a third party.

Some of these are fairly simple to understand – fulfilment of a contract and satisfying a legal obligation – and others are quite specific, from vital interests (covering for example medical data where dealt with by hospitals) and the public interest tasks of many authorities. In the context of the internet, the two categories that are the most important – and the most misunderstood and misused – are consent and 'legitimate interests'.

Consent on the internet is in practice largely illusionary, whether it is acquired through pages and pages of 'terms and conditions' that are scrolled past without reading and then 'OK' clicked without thinking, or through giving your thumbprint on your phone just to get an app to download. Sometimes consent is assumed by the act of using a website – do you consent to Google processing your search data when you type something in the search box? Are you told how the data will be used? The GDPR refers to explicit and informed consent, but even that is also often misleading: are you really informed by being presented with large amounts of information that you are highly unlikely to read and even if you do read you are unlikely to understand? Even if you do understand, can you understand the implications?

Legitimate interests may be even more of a challenge. The ICO sets out a three-part test that should be applied if you wish to use it as a basis:

1. identify a legitimate interest;
2. show that the processing is necessary to achieve it; and
3. balance it against the individual's interests, rights and freedoms.

While this test may seem sensible, it leaves the decisions very much in the hands of the processor and the benefit of any doubt as to the relevant balances will only really go in one direction.

Whichever justification for gathering or processing data is used, the aforementioned principles still apply: making the purpose of data gathering and processing clear, keeping the uses consistent with that purpose, minimising the data and minimising the time it is kept, and keeping it securely and confidentially. The principles are sound, the practice much less clear. Data protection can and does very easily become a kind of 'tick box' exercise performed in a perfunctory way. Though the GDPR has raised the stakes – particularly in terms of the level of fines that are possible, which now have the potential to be large enough to hurt even giants like Google and Facebook – it is not really much of a protection against the many uses of data that effectively but less directly infringe on our privacy as discussed throughout this book.

Enforcement is another real problem. The various Data Protection Authorities ('DPAs'), of which the UK's ICO is an example, tend to be poorly funded, poorly resourced and unable to keep up with the huge changes happening in the internet world. They often rely on 'self-reporting' by companies who have problems with data – the GDPR requires them to report a data breach within 72 hours of becoming aware of it – rather than having any capability to discover them. They tend to be reactive and to deal with problems after they happen – big data breaches rather than policies and practices that infringe upon our privacy and autonomy. Data protection itself, as it focuses on *personal* data and the harms that can come to individuals as a result of issues with their personal data, misses the bigger societal harms that do not relate to specific individuals directly. Data protection, at least as it is currently set out and used, is at best a limited tool to address only a small subset of the problems with internet privacy.

The second important part of the legal protections for privacy are the various forms of oversight built into surveillance law. These come in a number of categories: warrants required before intercepting data, the need for senior officers to authorise access to communications data, oversight bodies auditing records and producing annual reports, governmental oversight and rights to challenge actions by the authorities through courts and tribunals.

For the IPA, there is an Investigatory Powers Commissioner (a senior judge who together with other Judicial Commissioners deals with warrants), two advisory oversight bodies (the Technical Advisory Board and the Technology Advisory Panel) and the Investigatory Powers Tribunal, a court that adjudicates disputes and challenges. Together these are intended to produce accountability and ensure that the relevant agencies and authorities do not overreach. The extent to which they actually work is another matter: the historical record is not exactly promising. Before the Snowden revelations, the security and intelligence agencies had never lost a case at the Investigatory Powers Tribunal, though it had operated since 2000. Nonetheless, this does provide some degree of protection from government intrusion.

Protection from criminal invasions of privacy comes through the Computer Misuse Act 1990 in the UK and its equivalents around the world. The Convention on Cybercrime, an international convention signed up to by over 60 countries, requires those countries to have equivalent laws and to cooperate with other countries in investigating and prosecuting cyber criminals. Actions criminalised by these laws include illegally accessing computer systems and data, interfering with computer systems, making and distributing viruses and performing 'denial of service' and 'distributed denial of service' attacks – where large numbers of devices connect to the same systems or servers to overload them and force them out of action. Privacy-invasive actions like accessing data, installing spyware or disabling security measures come within the remit of these laws and are illegal. As with data protection the problem is not the law so much as detection and enforcement. The regularity with which there are significant data breaches is testament to the challenge. The law is, at least at present, a poor protector of privacy.

What could and should be better than the law is technological protection. There are various strands to this: the encryption of content of messages, websites and other traffic, the use of virtual private networks (VPNs) which make it harder for observers to determine your location and identity, and the securing of the devices that we connect to the internet itself and much more. Just as those who wish to invade privacy find ways to intervene at every stage of our connection, privacy protective technology can intervene at all those stages to attempt at least to stymie those invasions.

It is a kind of arms race between hackers and developers, between governments and those working to protect individuals – and of course those trying to evade government interference for both good reasons and bad. It is often difficult to tell who is winning that race, particularly as it mostly goes on in the shadows and there are conflicting motivations from both sides to present themselves as winning or losing. Governments sometimes want it to look as though the internet is full of all-powerful rogues, to justify their latest plans for intrusion, and sometimes want it to seem as though those plans have been succeeding, making the internet safe for all.

Neither is likely to be true, though some developments do tip the balance significantly. The most important of these surround encryption, the single most important and widely applicable way to protect privacy on the internet. Encryption is vital to both privacy and security, and government attempts to undermine it are regular and deeply disappointing. Rather, governments should be supporting and encouraging the development of stronger encryption and its deployment throughout the internet. Sadly, that seems far from the route that they currently wish to follow.

4

what should we do?

Sometimes it seems as though there is very little we can really do. Privacy is dead, we are told, and we might as well accept that. When privacy on the internet is looked at in any depth it is easy to find yourself agreeing with that rather depressing analysis – but it would be a mistake to do so for a number of reasons. The first is that the consequences of accepting the death of privacy are so significant. If we give up on *internet* privacy, we might as well give up on *all* privacy as the internet pervades almost every aspect of our lives and it is far from clear that we are ready for that. History shows, no matter what some might say, that we have always needed and wanted privacy and have fought for it when we have properly understood that it was under threat. The biggest problem right now is a lack of understanding of the consequences of our failure to protect privacy. When we do grasp this, history suggests that there will be action.

The signs are that we *are* starting to do something about it. Privacy has moved from being an obscure subject for conspiracy theorists to headline news on a regular basis, a discussion point for politicians and, at times at least, a selling point for companies. Even Facebook now markets itself as taking privacy very seriously, though in many ways it is the worst culprit of all in terms of privacy invasion and in particular its impact. Keeping privacy in the headlines is crucial as it puts pressure on those who can have a significant impact on our privacy.

That works in a number of ways. First, it provides an incentive for companies to take privacy more seriously, to keep themselves out of these negative headlines. Privacy-friendly products and services that are user-friendly and attractive – and at prices that mean they will sell – are a key part of any positive route forward. Positive headlines mean that those who develop privacy-protective technology are more likely to find a market for it – and could incentivise that development. This is already happening. Apple, for example, has been both developing new privacy-friendly technology and making it a selling point. Apple's 2019 iPhone software, iOS 13, includes a raft of new privacy features including the capability to strip away location metadata from photos when uploading and alerts when software tries to use features like Bluetooth to track you.

Second, it means that politicians are also more likely to be persuadable in the right direction – and the role of politicians is critical here. Third, it means that people will become more aware of the issues, and hence more likely to use privacy-protective technology and less likely to engage in fundamentally privacy-damaging actions which harm others as well as themselves. They are also less likely to support politicians who drive privacy-invasive policies or companies which build privacy-invasive business models.

When looking at what we should be doing about internet privacy, the first thing to emphasise is what we should *not* be doing because a good deal of the time what governments in particular are pushing is not just ineffective but directly counterproductive. Some policies are in practice the *worst* things they could be doing not just for privacy but for security and for both personal and societal freedom. Two stand out in particular: real names and encryption.

'Real' names should be avoided

Whenever there is any kind of 'nastiness' on social media – trolling, hate speech, cyber bullying, 'revenge porn' – there are immediate calls to force people to use their real names. It is seen as some kind of panacea, based in part on the idea that 'hiding' behind a false name makes people feel free to behave badly and the related idea that they would be ashamed to do so if they were forced to reveal their real names. 'Sunlight is the best disinfectant' is a compelling argument on the surface but when examined more closely it is not just likely to be ineffective but counterproductive, discriminatory and with the side effect of putting many different groups of people at significant risk. Moreover, there are already both technical and legal methods to discover who is behind an online account without the negative side effects.

The empirical evidence, counterintuitive though it might seem, suggests that when forced to use their real names internet trolls actually become more rather than less aggressive. There are a number of possible explanations for this. It might be seen as a 'badge of honour'. Sometimes being a troll is something to boast about – and showing your real identity gives you kudos. Having to use your real name might actually free you from the shackles of wanting to hide. Perhaps it just makes trolls feel there's nothing more to hide.

Whatever the explanation, forcing real names on people does not seem to stem the tide of nastiness. Platforms where real names are required – Facebook is the most obvious here – are conspicuously *not* free from harmful material, bullying and trolling. The internet is no longer anything like the place where 'nobody knows you're a dog', even if you are operating under a pseudonym. There are many technological ways to know all kinds of thing about someone on the internet regardless of 'real-names' policies. The authorities can break down most forms of pseudonymity and anonymity when they need to, while others can use a particular legal mechanism, the Norwich Pharmacal Order, to require the disclosure of information about an apparently anonymous individual from service providers when needed.

Even more importantly, requirements for real names can be deeply damaging to many people, as they provide the link between the online and 'real-world' identities. People operating under oppressive regimes – it should be no surprise that the Chinese government is very keen on real-names policies – are perhaps the most obvious, but whistle-blowers, people in positions of responsibility like police officers or doctors who want to share important insider stories, victims of domestic violence, young people who quite reasonably might not want their parents to know what they are doing, people with illnesses who wish to find out more about those illnesses, are just a start.

There are some specific groups who can and do suffer discrimination as a result of real-names policies: people with names that identify their religion or ethnicity, for a start, and indeed their gender. Transgender people suffer particularly badly – who defines what their 'real' name is, and how? Real names can also allow trolls and bullies to find and identify their victims – damaging exactly the people that the policies are intended to protect. It is not a coincidence that a common trolling tactic is *doxxing* – releasing *documents* about someone so that they can be targeted for abuse in the real world.

When looked at in the round, rather than requiring real names we should be looking to enshrine the right to pseudonymity online. It is a critical protection for many of exactly the people who need protection. Sadly, just as with encryption, it is much more likely that the authorities will push in exactly the wrong direction on this.

Encryption matters

When the then Home Secretary Amber Rudd said that 'real people' did not need end-to-end encryption she was echoing one of the most familiar and fundamental arguments against privacy: that good people don't need privacy and bad people don't deserve privacy, so no one should have privacy. She was also pushing the opposite of the truth: the people she describes as 'real' are exactly those who need end-to-end encryption, for their security, their privacy and their freedom. Encryption, when properly done, is one of the few ways to protect the contents of a message that really works – and it is the 'real' people, who need it the most.

They are the ones who unlike the rich and powerful don't have many alternatives to the mainstream communications systems at their disposal, who unlike the serious criminals and hackers don't have the expertise or resources to create their own forms of encrypted or otherwise protected communications. They are the victims of scammers, the ones likely to be exploitatively profiled and targeted commercially and politically, and the ones whose rights to protest and to dissent need to be protected.

Rather than seeking by word, deed and law to undermine encryption and other technological protections for privacy, politicians should be encouraging its development and supporting its use. The demands for 'back doors' or 'breakable' encryption should be resisted firmly and clearly. As computer scientists have repeatedly explained, there is no such thing as a back door that works only for the 'good guys' – even if it is possible to identify who the 'good guys' are. Governments change. Authorities that you feel you can trust can be replaced by those you certainly can't – and if you've built a back door for one, you've built it for them all.

It is not just encryption but the whole of our approach to surveillance that needs a thorough rethink. The miscast ideas that underpin the debate need to be challenged. The downplaying of privacy is particularly prevalent in the surveillance debate as is the attempt to ignore the potential risks that are *increased* by state surveillance. At the same time, the effectiveness of that surveillance in achieving its stated goals is overstated. The result of this is that surveillance is presented as far more attractive than it really is, and laws such as the Investigatory Powers Act 2016 are passed despite their deep flaws and overreach, from the farce that is the 'internet connection record' to the continuing and counterproductive war on encryption.

Upgrading politics

Part of the reason that this happens is a failure of politics – or to be more precise a failure of our politicians. It is not just in the UK that politicians struggle to understand not just how the internet works from a technological perspective but most of the issues that surround its use. Hearings of parliamentary committees and debates in Parliament demonstrate all too often that the politicians do not even understand the laws that they are responsible for creating and passing.

This needs to change. We need an upgrade in our politicians. This starts with questioning and challenging politicians more about how much they understand – and trying to bring about the election of more who understand the technology and how it is used. We also need to do what we can to ensure that those appointed to ministerial and shadow ministerial positions understand not just the technology but their responsibility over it.

Better politics should mean better decisions about the internet – from a willingness to take advice from genuine experts to an acceptance of complexity and the consequential resistance to superficial but counter-productive solutions. It could mean a bolder approach to regulation: data protection, though limited in its impact at present, has the potential to be far more effective if it is broadened in scope and the regulators are given the resources that they need to enforce it more quickly and effectively. Stronger regulation could mean being more active and interventionist, rather than reactive and 'soft touch', making some of the more egregious practices illegal and daring to challenge certain 'accepted practice' as actually unacceptable. The behavioural advertising industry is a prime example.

Conversely, worse politics means worse decisions about the internet. Politicians who take advantage of the manipulative opportunities offered by privacy invasions are unlikely to take measures against them, while those in thrall to corporate lobbyists will be highly resistant to the necessary measures to restrict the power of the giants, let alone break them up. Too often there has been a cosy relationship between politicians and the big guns of the internet. When the contentious 'right to be forgotten' was being discussed in 2014, for example, though all the other hearings before the House of Lords Committee researching it were in public, Google was somehow granted a private, closed hearing. It was not a surprise when the report that emerged from that inquiry ended up taking pretty much precisely Google's line on the matter.

Politicians whose main contact with issues related to surveillance is through the security and intelligence services find it very difficult to understand the bigger picture or take a balanced view of the subject. This is a toxic combination as far as internet privacy is concerned and makes the prospects of radical solutions from politicians sadly extremely remote. Ultimately, that will only change as and when politicians see there is a political benefit to supporting privacy – and *that* will only happen if voters start to show that they understand *and care* about privacy.

What can we do?

That brings us to our role as 'ordinary' people – to be more precise, our many roles, as consumers, as citizens, as voters. To a significant degree, as the various examples used throughout this book have shown, though our privacy has been eroded by stealth, we have allowed this erosion through complacency.

We need to be smarter about privacy in a whole lot of ways. We should use privacy-friendly technology when we can: VPNs, ad-blockers, encrypted message and email services, and more. Turn location services off on your phone whenever you can. Avoid online quizzes and questionnaires – they're always primarily for data gathering and profiling – particularly those on Facebook and other social media services. Where there is a choice, we should use systems not owned or operated by the internet giants – because the aggregation of data and concentration of power is one of the biggest threats to our privacy, as we should be increasingly aware.

This is just one of the ways in which we need to be willing to learn more about what is going on – and to think more about the consequences of our actions not just for ourselves but for the rest of society. It is not only the politicians that need to listen to the experts more, but all of us. That in turn puts pressure on those of us who *do* understand at least some of what is going on to try to help others to learn. Far better education about privacy on the internet is a key part of the story and not just for children: despite what is often said, young people may be both better at protecting their privacy and at avoiding the consequences of privacy failures.

The old adage that there is no such thing as a free lunch has a great deal of truth to it over the internet. Much of what we are presented with *appears* to be free: we need to be more cynical and thoughtful about what is really going on. One of the more common 'bargains' that is made is to sacrifice privacy for convenience. When this is combined with shiny new tech, particularly tech that looks and feels like the kind of thing seen in science fiction films, it is hard to resist. The attraction of the 'internet of things' is based very much on this and it is a false bargain to a great extent: the privacy-related consequences of filling homes with 'smart' devices are barely acknowledged let alone understood. What is true for the internet of things is true for a raft of other areas. The trend to give away DNA for dubious information about heritage or ancestry works in the same way, as do games like Pokemon Go that map movements and behaviour patterns in exchange for playing a fairly trivial game.

The most critical of these seemingly attractive but on balance destructive phenomena is social media, and Facebook in particular. As things currently stand, the single most important thing that any individual can do to protect their privacy and autonomy is to remove themselves from Facebook and to encourage their friends, relatives and businesses to do likewise. The reasons for this should be apparent from many of the examples in this book: Facebook's whole business model is based around manipulation through the use of personal data.

That this has been manifested *politically* in recent years should focus our minds, because political deception and exploitation seem particularly egregious and hit at our very concept of freedom. The manipulation Facebook not just allows but positively encourages, however, works in all aspects of our lives. Whether it is governments trying to 'head off' legitimate protest or lobbyists surreptitiously spreading disinformation about climate change, Facebook makes it possible in ways that previously would have been unimaginable. A mechanism that idealists thought could 'democratise' the world has in practice enabled exactly the opposite. The question that needs to be asked is whether the positives that come from the way that Facebook works – what it brings to freedom of speech, the tools that it provides for coordination, organisation and enjoyment of groups and communities and much more – are possible without the negatives that its business model imposes upon it. Can there be a form of Facebook that helps our communications and supports our businesses and interests without also leaving us open to manipulation and exploitation and undermining our democratic systems? Given the nature of Facebook's business model it is hard to see a way, and most of the ideas put forward by Zuckerberg in particular appear designed much more to protect that business model than to address the underlying issues, but the positives about Facebook do mean that it is worth considering. The opposite, however, that we need to do everything we can to disentangle ourselves from Facebook, should be taken very seriously too.

Facebook is not the only villain of this piece. YouTube can spread fake news just as effectively, with 'false flag' videos making it to the top of trending lists after mass shootings in the United States again and again as their curation algorithms are gamed by those who seek to mislead. Twitter is used to spread it further – both through targeting that relies on profiling based on private information. Google, which owns YouTube, has an empire in many ways as expansive and powerful as Facebook's and which of them has the most data on us is largely a moot point: both have far more data on us than is healthy for our privacy and autonomy and for the future of our democracies.

Disentangling oneself from Facebook is not easy. Facebook is designed to be user-friendly and convenient as well as being free. Being on Facebook is now so much the norm that many aspects of many people's social and working lives are organised through Facebook and Facebook alone. That may make it effectively impossible for many to leave but the impact that Facebook has can be reduced. Cutting down what you do on Facebook is the first step. Try not to use Facebook as your source of news. Avoid logging on to other services through Facebook. When you play games, do it directly rather than through Facebook or other social media. Try sharing fewer photographs – and when you do, use something other than Facebook or Instagram (which is owned by Facebook) and private and encrypted platforms if possible. Do not use the 'like' button on a website for anything – the like button not only is a self-profiling tool but also collects and transmits a whole raft of your data to Facebook. Try not to be 'friends' with people that you are not really friends with. Find other ways to do as many of the things that you currently do through Facebook as you can – and don't just shift to one alternative for everything; try to diversify and use different services for different things. Reducing dependence on one platform also helps protect not only your privacy but that of others, as it cuts down the data aggregation and weakens the potential for analysis and profiling.

Having said all of that, though all of this is possible it is far from easy. The very things that make Facebook the most dangerous – the way that it concentrates data, profiles in so many different ways, the way that 'everyone' is on Facebook so it can monitor whole populations – are what make it so attractive. It would take a gargantuan effort to wean ourselves off Facebook. If we can find a way, there is a great deal to gain not just in societal terms but as individuals, as it should reduce the chances of becoming victims of trolls and scammers, or of being duped by fake news and other misinformation. Conversely, if we cannot find a way, there is an enormous amount to lose both as individuals and as a society.

Breaking up the giants

It should not be up to us, as ordinary people, as citizens and consumers, to find our way through this quagmire. It is unreasonable to expect people to understand let alone act to deal with what are in essence societal problems on a mass scale. This is where politicians and regulators need to be the boldest. Rather than scratching at the surface of the issues, dealing piecemeal with a much bigger problem, they need to grasp the nettle and be willing to take on seriously the internet giants – Facebook in particular, but also Google, Amazon and others. We need to find a way to reduce their power – power which they wield not just through their influence over the relevant markets but through their vast data resources, data gathering capabilities, data analytical power and direct access to people. All of these need to be considered together and all need to be addressed.

That means being willing not just to block future takeovers but to go a step further and break the giants up. Facebook was allowed to acquire both Instagram and WhatsApp despite the impact that each had both on the power of the company and its ability to aggregate and analyse data, to profile and target individuals and to manipulate communities. The failure to prevent these acquisitions has at least been partially acknowledged for what it is: a failure. In Germany, the competition authorities have at least tried to stop the sharing of data between Facebook and WhatsApp. This needs to be taken much further and ultimately the only solution is likely to be a break-up of many of the internet giants, unless they can find a *genuine* way to change how they operate. Whether it is possible for Facebook to evolve into something that does not rely on data gathering, profiling and targeting, that pays more than lip-service to privacy, without being forced to do so, is a big question. Break-up seems likely to be the only practical solution.

Quite how it is to be managed is another matter, particularly as the companies have immensely powerful lobbyists and legal teams that will fight tooth and nail to retain their power and protect not only their businesses but also their business models. Data protection law has some of the keys. In particular, the idea that data should be minimised is one that should be focused on rather than sidestepped or ignored. It is not enough, however, just to tinker at the edges, leaving the underlying problem untouched.

Competition law has some more of the keys, dealing with market dominance and the issues that spring from it – but the tendency to focus on our role as consumers, and on specific harms, generally financial, to individuals, limits its ability to deal with the bigger picture. Combining data protection with competition law might be a good starting point, but that is all it is – a starting point. We need much more if we are to find a positive way out of this before too much damage is done to be repairable.

5

conclusions

It is easy to be despondent about internet privacy. We rely on the internet in a way that we have never relied on a single form of technology at any time in the past. We need it for our communications, as our route to information, as part of our working lives and our personal lives. It is how we find our entertainment and how we access news. It is where the media functions and where politics functions. Our freedom in almost all aspects of the 'real' world is tied to our freedom on the internet – and that freedom is dependent on our ability to protect our privacy, as the many examples discussed in this book should make clear.

At the same time, as we have seen, our privacy is under threat from multiple directions. Businesses, governments, political pressure groups, criminals and many more see opportunities in monitoring us, in profiling us, in analysing us and in targeting us – and there are many ways that they can do this while we fail to protect our privacy sufficiently well. The technology and the business models that underpin the internet, as described in the 'what do we know?' chapter actively support this monitoring, data gathering, profiling and targeting.

Even more concerning, the trends going forward seem generally negative. Governments seem to be keener on surveillance day by day and continue to pursue fundamentally misguided policies such as undermining encryption. Facebook and Google seem to tighten their stranglehold of the internet and are expanding their services into emerging areas such as artificial intelligence and virtual reality, dominating the growing fields of health data and more. These key areas, building on the developing technologies of biometrics and the growth of the internet of things with all the issues that accompany them, all increase the risks and expand the threats to our privacy and autonomy in ways that at times seem inexorable.

There are, however, some signs of positivity, from the way that privacy issues are often headline news to the way that businesses now want to sell themselves as 'privacy-friendly' – even Facebook. People are starting to show that despite their embrace of the likes of Facebook they *do* care about privacy, otherwise privacy breaches would not make headline news and big commercial organisations would not be making privacy a selling point. Important legal cases have been won, many of them in very much David and Goliath forms, with small NGOs taking on governments and internet giants. The EU Data Retention Directive was invalidated as a result of an action brought by the tiny NGO Digital Rights Ireland, effectively run by one Irish academic, T. J. McIntyre, while the 'Safe Harbour Agreement', which enabled data transfers between the EU and the United States, was brought down by an action brought by an Austrian activist, Max Schrems. Actions from Privacy International, Liberty and others have forced the security and intelligence services in the UK to disclose much more about their practices than before. How we can help these positive signs to grow is vital, and supporting those NGOs and campaigners is a key part of this.

The most important thing of all is to find a way to change the paradigm. Privacy should be the default – and those that wish to invade it should need very good reasons to do so, and have to *prove* those reasons, rather than wait for our objections. Ultimately, it is a question of asking what kind of a future we want: one of convenience and control, or one of freedom and autonomy. I would like to think that we will choose the latter.

further reading and references

As this is very much a current topic and one that is developing all the time, a lot of the best information and resources concerning it are on the internet in the form of blogs as well as articles. The further reading set out here covers the background as well as some of the specific issues discussed in the book, but it is always good to follow the news and commentary as things develop. Some useful books on the nature of privacy are:

Westin, Alan (1967) *Privacy and Freedom*, Bodley Head.
Solove, Daniel (2008) *Understanding Privacy*, Harvard University Press.

The seminal 1890 article first setting out *The Right to Privacy*, is:

Warren, Samuel D. & Brandeis, Louis D. (1890) *The Right to Privacy*, *Harvard Law Review*, 4(5): 193–220.

The key human rights declarations are:

The Universal Declaration of Human Rights (1948) found at https://www.un.org/en/universal-declaration-human-rights/
The European Convention on Human Rights (1950) found at https://www.echr.coe.int/Pages/home.aspx?p=basictexts&c=
In a rather different direction and with very different status (and referred to in the text) there is John Perry Barlow's Declaration of the Independence of Cyberspace (1996), which can be found at https://www.eff.org/cyberspace-independence

A good and brief history of the internet can be found on the Internet Society website, at https://www.internetsociety.org/internet/history-internet/brief-history-internet/.

Overviews can also be found in the better textbooks on the law of the internet, most notably:

Reed, Chris (2004) *Internet Law: Text and Materials*, Cambridge University Press.

and

Murray, Andrew (2019) *Information Technology Law: The Law and Society*, 4th Edition, Oxford University Press.

On the internet *and* privacy there are a number of recent books to look at:

Bernal, Paul (2014) *Internet Privacy Rights: Rights to Protect Autonomy*, Cambridge University Press.
Bernal, Paul (2018) *The Internet, Warts and All: Free Speech, Privacy and Truth*, Cambridge University Press.
Cohen, Julie (2012) *Configuring the Networked Self: Law, Code, and the Play of Everyday Practice*, Yale University Press.
Nissenbaum, Helen (2010) *Privacy in Context: Technology, Policy, and the Integrity of Social Life*, Stanford Law Books.
Richards, Neil (2015) *Intellectual Privacy: Rethinking Civil Liberties in the Digital Age*, Oxford University Press.

On government and corporate surveillance respectively, two key resources are:

Solove, Daniel (2011) *Nothing to Hide: The False Tradeoff between Privacy and Security*, Yale University Press.
Zuboff, Shoshana (2018) *The Age of Surveillance Capitalism: The Fight for a Human Future at the New Frontier of Power*, Profile.

A key campaign on this subject, which uses the work of Bruce Schneier, is 'Reform Corporate Surveillance' found at http://reformcorporatesurveillance.com

On why the war on encryption is such a bad idea, the definitive report is:

Abelson, Harold, Anderson, Ross, Bellovin, Steven, Benaloh, Josh, Blaze, Matt, Whitfield, Diffie et al. (2015) *Keys Under Doormats: Mandating Insecurity by Requiring Government Access to All Data and Communications*, Computer Science and Artificial Intelligence Laboratory Technical Report, MIT-CSAIL-TR-2015-026, https://dspace.mit.edu/bitstream/handle/1721.1/97690/MIT-CSAIL-TR-2015-026.pdf

Some of the research into profiling by Facebook, the potential impact on voting and so forth:

Bergstrom, Carl & Bak-Coleman, Joseph (2019) Information gerrymandering in social networks skews collective decision-making, *Nature*, 573: 40–41, doi: 10.1038/d41586-019-02562-z

Kosinski, Michal, Stillwell, David & Graepel, Thore (2013) Private traits and attributes are predictable from digital records of human behavior, *PNAS*, 110(15): 5802–5805, https://doi.org/10.1073/pnas.1218772110 (covering the Facebook 'likes' study).

Kramer, Adam D.I., Guillory, Jamie E. & Hancock, Jeffrey T. (2014) Experimental evidence of massive-scale emotional contagion through social networks, *PNAS*, 111 (24): 8788-8790; first published June 2, 2014 https://doi.org/10.1073/pnas.1320040111

Kreiss, Daniel & McGregor, Shannon (2018) Technology firms shape political communication: The work of Microsoft, Facebook, Twitter, and Google with campaigns during the 2016 US presidential cycle, *Political Communication*, 35(2): 155–177, DOI: 10.1080/10584609.2017.1364814

Kristensen, Jakob, Albrechtsen, Thomas, Dahl-Nielsen, Emil, Jensen, Michael, Skovrind, Magnus & Bornakke, Tobias (2017) Parsimonious data: How a single Facebook like predicts voting behavior in multiparty systems, *PLOS ONE*, 12(9): e0184562., https://doi.org/10.1371/journal.pone.0184562

On real names and trolling:

Rost, Katja, Stahel, Lea & Frey, Bruno (2016) Digital social norm enforcement: Online firestorms in social media, *PLOS ONE*, 11(6): e0155923, DOI: 10.1371/journal.pone.0155923

Other books and articles referred to in the text include:

Calo, M. Ryan (2011) The boundaries of privacy harm, *Indiana Law Journal*, 86: 1131.

Weigend, Andreas (2017) *Data for the People: How to Make Our Post-Privacy Economy Work for You*. Basic Books, New York.

Privacy and related NGOs

One of the recommendations in the conclusion to this book is that we need to support NGOs that work in privacy and related fields. Some of the best of these in the UK and US are:

Amnesty International www.amnesty.org.uk

Big Brother Watch https://bigbrotherwatch.org.uk

Digital Rights Ireland www.digitalrights.ie

EDRi https://edri.org

The Electronic Frontier Foundation www.eff.org

further reading and references

Liberty www.libertyhumanrights.org.uk

medConfidential https://medconfidential.org

The Open Rights Group www.openrightsgroup.org

Privacy International https://privacyinternational.org

Statewatch www.statewatch.org

There are privacy-related NGOs in most countries around the world. Organisations such as EDRi, Privacy International and the Electronic Frontier Foundation will be able to help you to find one relevant to your local circumstances.

index

advertising 1, 21, 35, 38, 39, 41, 68
ad-blockers 33
algorithms 25, 37, 39, 40, 41, 70
anonymity 16–17, 18, 65
artificial intelligence (AI) 26, 44, 73

bias 25–6, 41
big data 24–6, 37–8
biometrics 46–8
browser fingerprinting 33, 36, 47–8

care.data 45–6
confidentiality 4–5, 8, 9, 44, 46
criminals 9, 27, 56–7, 61–2

data protection 11, 51, 58–61, 67–8, 72
DNA 48, 69
encryption 2, 8, 55, 62, 66–7

Facebook 1, 3, 7, 5, 12, 22–3, 26, 27, 28–9, 31, 38, 39–40, 47, 51, 52, 53, 63, 65, 69–71, 71–2, 73–4
facial recognition 47

GDPR 58–60, 61
Google 3, 5, 20–2, 23, 28–9, 31, 39, 41, 45, 50, 52, 60, 68, 70, 72, 73–4

harm 11–12, 34–5
health data 44–6, 50
human rights law 4, 7, 57

Information Commissioner's Office (ICO) 58, 60
internet of things 2, 18, 35, 48–51, 69
Investigatory Powers Act (IPA) 54–5, 61, 67

location data 42–4, 47, 50

mobile phones 19, 43, 47, 64

NSA 27–8

Orbitz 36, 37–8

personalisation 22, 36, 37, 40, 41, 53
police 4, 26, 54, 56, 65
political data 51–3
profiling 2, 12, 21–2, 23, 29, 34–5, 36, 37, 40–1, 51, 52–3
pseudonymity 18, 65, 66

racism 40
real names 2, 20, 64–6
right to be forgotten 68

search 20–2
social networking 22–4
smart devices 2, 18, 35, 48–51, 69
Snowden revelations 1, 11, 27–8, 31, 54
surveillance 2, 5, 11, 26–9, 54–6, 61, 67

tailoring 22, 36, 37, 41, 52, 53
targeting 21, 22, 29, 40, 41, 52–3, 37
trolls 2, 20, 65, 66, 71

Virtual Private Networks ('VPNs') 62

wearables 45, 50
World Wide Web 2, 20

YouTube 70